D0881166

Moving on After Trauma

'Michael Scott has penned a thoughtful, accessible and easily readable book for trauma survivors. It will act as an excellent guide for survivors and their families and can be used by the individual instead of therapy, as they await therapy or as a workbook to accompany their therapy. It is grounded in the Cognitive Behavioural Psychotherapy (CBT) approach and flows easily from helping people understand their experiences and problems after trauma, to managing then treating their problems and symptoms. In giving individuals practical solutions and a range of options it allows control to be regained. *Moving on After Trauma* offers options for the reader to do exactly that: move on following traumatic experience.'

Dr Alastair Hull, Consultant Psychiatrist in
Psychotherapy, NHS Tayside

'Michael Scott has produced an excellent book that should be of immense value to sufferers of PTSD and their relatives. I particularly like its clear link with theory and evidence and it is replete with useful case examples. Scott's extensive clinical experience in dealing with these problems is evident in his thorough and sensitive handling of the topic. Packed full of strategies and tips for dealing effectively with trauma symptoms and associated problems this book should be at the top of a sufferer's self-help list.'

Adrian Wells, Professor of Clinical and Experimental
Psychopathology, University of Manchester, UK

'This valuable guide explains the puzzling and disturbing symptoms of post-traumatic stress disorder and what to do about them. There is a wealth of practical wisdom, supported by many practical examples, that cannot fail to inform and help trauma victims and their families.'

Chris Brewin, Professor of Clinical Psychology,
University College London.

The effects of extreme trauma can continue to be emotionally devastating. *Moving on After Trauma* offers hope, providing survivors, family members and friends with a roadmap for managing emotional, relationship, physical and legal obstacles to recovery. Dr Scott details examples of the strategies used by twenty characters who have recovered and the survivor (with or without the help of a family member, friend or counsellor) is encouraged to identify with one or more of them and follow in their footsteps.

Michael J. Scott is a Consultant Psychologist specialising in the assessment and treatment of post-traumatic stress disorder. Dr Scott is the author of five textbooks including *Counselling for Post-Traumatic Stress Disorder*, now in its third edition. He divides his time between treating clients, research, medico-legal work, writing and External Examiner duties for the MSc in Cognitive and Behavioural Psychotherapies at the University of Chester.

Moving on After Trauma
A guide for survivors, family and friends

Michael J. Scott

Routledge
Taylor & Francis Group

LONDON AND NEW YORK

First published 2008
by Routledge
27 Church Lane, Hove, East Sussex, BN3 2FA

Simultaneously published in the USA and Canada
by Routledge
270 Madison Avenue, New York, NY 10016

Routledge is an imprint of the Taylor & Francis Group, an Informa business

Copyright © 2008 Michael J. Scott

Typeset in Century Schoolbook by
RefineCatch Limited, Bungay, Suffolk
Printed and bound in Great Britain by
MPG Books Ltd, Bodmin, Cornwall
Paperback cover design by Lisa Dynan

This publication has been produced with paper manufactured to strict
environmental standards and with pulp derived from sustainable forests.

British Library Cataloguing in Publication Data
A catalogue record for this book is available from the British Library

Library of Congress Cataloging-in-Publication Data

Scott, Michael J., 1948–
   Moving on after trauma : a guide for survivors, family and
friends / Michael J. Scott.
      p. cm.
   Includes bibliographical references and index.
   ISBN 978-0-415-40962-9 (hardback) – ISBN 978-0-415-40963-6
(pbk)   1. Post-traumatic stress disorder – Patients –
Rehabilitation.   2. Crisis intervention (Mental health services).
I. Title.
   RC552.P67S355 2007
616.85'21–dc22

                              2007010441

                              ISBN: 978-0-415-40962-9 (hbk)
                              ISBN: 978-0-415-40963-6 (pbk)

Preface

This book is for all those who have been traumatised (and their relatives and friends) whether it is through a serious car accident, assault as an adult or child, accident at work or as a victim of a natural or man-made disaster. The book offers a roadmap from preoccupation with the traumatic memory to reinvesting in life. With the aid of simple drawings, the author explains the problems caused by the maintenance of an overactive alarm post trauma and, importantly, how it can be reset. This is a companion volume to the author's best-selling *Counselling for Post-Traumatic Stress Disorder* for mental health professionals, now in its third edition.

Contents

Preface   viii

Introduction: how to use this book   1

1 **What's happening to me?**   5
2 **Making sense of my reactions**   25
3 **Will I get better?**   34
4 **What works?**   39
5 **Resetting the alarm**   46
6 **Better ways of handling the traumatic memory**   63
7 **Restoring relationships**   83
8 **Managing mood**   94
9 **Managing sleep and pain**   119
10 **Old baggage, new trauma**   133
11 **Managing additional disorders**   138
12 **Children and adolescents**   151
13 **Justice**   158
14 **Getting further help**   165
15 **Guidance for professionals using this book**   169

Appendix A: Screening for PTSD   173
Appendix B: Unreliable diagnosis   175
Appendix C: DSM-IV-TR diagnostic criteria for PTSD, depression and panic disorder   176
References   182
Index   185

Introduction

How to use this book

If you are reading this book to get some guidance on how to move on after your major trauma, you may well have some problems with concentration. Many trauma victims are hyper-alert for danger, as if on sentry duty in a war zone, and this makes concentration on reading difficult. You may wish to avoid reading anything connected with your trauma but this is counterbalanced by a curiosity that has led you to read so far. In these pages you are likely to meet characters who sound all too familiar and there will be a strong tendency to want to run away, but if you follow their story through you will see that there is hope.

If concentration is a problem for you, probably the best way forward is to

- budget to read in very small doses, maybe just ten minutes
- make a written note of an important point as you read
- avoid being overwhelmed by controlling the dose of exposure to anything that you read that might be upsetting
- share with someone close to you what seems important – encourage them to read the book
- reread what you have read the next day.

If you have been traumatised it is quite possible to read the words on a page but then not be able to recall what you have read. Read in very small doses, just for say ten minutes. To make sure what you have read sticks, summarise important points in a sentence or two (on paper or in your head) before reading further. After ten minutes change gear – have a break, have a cup of tea, go for a walk or have a shower. You may fear being overwhelmed or 'swallowed up' if you go anywhere near anything related to your trauma, but in reading this book you are in control. Go as gently with yourself as you would with a toddler who is afraid of water in the swimming pool and you will be OK. Discussing what you have read with someone close to you can help clarify what you have read and also help build a bridge of understanding. Revisiting what you have read the next day helps clarify what you read: while asleep your mind will have been working on the material and when you return to it you will probably get more out of it.

In Chapter 1 you will be introduced to twenty people who have been traumatised by differing events, and who suffer from a variety of disorders. You might find that you identify with some individuals much more than others, and by using the index at the back of this book, you might want to track how they resolve their difficulties. Alternatively you may of course simply read the book from cover to cover.

For friends and family

It is a struggle for almost all trauma victims to try to explain to friends and family the impact the incident or incidents have had on them. When you can't explain something to yourself, how can you explain it to others? What you might do is to get a friend or family member to read the book or at least those parts of the book that seem important to you. In this way you will share a common language about your difficulties and they might better appreciate that you are not just being an awkward, cantankerous *@%!

If you are a relative or a friend of a trauma survivor, this book will give you a map of the world that they seem to inhabit now. It will seem a strange land but with the aid of the analogies in Chapter 2, you will be able to understand the terrain and can share this with them. Trauma victims find it an enormous relief when someone quite clearly understands what they are going through. Importantly, in reading the succeeding chapters, you will be better able to help them navigate their return. Realistically however the journey is likely to take several months, and it is invariably a case of two steps forward and one step back. The victim will need your encouragement that backward steps are par for the course, need to be budgeted for, and that the show is still on the road.

Sometimes more than one family member has been affected by the trauma and each can be an unwitting obstacle to the other moving on. When a number of family members have been affected, there is particularly likely to be a conspiracy of silence about the tragedy born of a fear of upsetting further the other victims. If you are a victim of a trauma who knows others who are similarly traumatised, while it would be helpful to encourage them to read this book, you can also powerfully help them by modelling for them the strategies for gradually re-engaging in life described here. We probably learn more from watching others in action than from any words.

If you are reading this book and were not directly traumatised yourself, but a number of family members or friends were, you can encourage those affected to read the book and/or try out the strategies. It can be particularly challenging if you are trying to help more than one victim. Following the tragedy, family beliefs may have developed about the importance of not talking about the incident or of the pointlessness of activity; these unhelpful ideas can sabotage engaging with the recommendations contained in this book or engagement in psychological treatment. In order to remove these saboteurs you may want to adopt the style of the TV detective Columbo, who with an air of bemused befuddlement might say 'Has not doing things since the incident worked?' or 'How do you know it would not be better if you did "X", if you have not tried it?' or 'If you are not putting anything into life how can you expect to get anything out?', then beating a hasty retreat and leaving the person to mull over the matter rather than get into an argument

As an aid to counselling

If you feel that you have not been helped at all or only to a very limited extent by the professional help you have had from a counsellor or a therapist, you can point out what you have found useful or interesting in what you have read in this book and this may lead to a redirection and re-energising of the counselling. In Chapter 15 of this book there is guidance for professionals as to how they might use this book as an adjunct to their counselling. Very detailed guidance for professionals is given in *Counselling for Post-Traumatic Stress Disorder*, which I co-authored with Professor Steve Stradling, now in its third edition (Scott and Stradling 2006).

1

What's happening to me?

'I am not the same person, frightened of my own shadow, don't want to know anyone or do anything, like a bear with a sore head!' If this sounds familiar, the chances are that you have experienced an extreme event, e.g. serious car crash or assault. The likelihood is that the extreme trauma is dictating how you think about yourself and the world around you. Events that happened before the extreme trauma, such as being present at the birth of your first child, do not seem to count any more. You have a crisis of identity.

Trauma has a way of putting 'danger signs' (hyper-arousal) on anything vaguely related to the incident.

Sam was a car driver involved in a serious road traffic accident. Afterwards not only was he afraid to travel as a passenger in a car, but also he became very anxious when his young children were clambering over the furniture at home. Needless to say, Sam's wife Maria was not best pleased with his growling at the children over such minor matters and their relationship had become strained since the accident. He felt she just did not understand but then he could not explain his reactions to her or his lack of warmth (emotional numbness). Sam had always prided himself on being a rational, very much in control person, and now he felt he was losing it. His head was saying one thing, e.g. 'of course it is safe to drive to work', but when he did so his gut reactions were that something catastrophic was going to happen and he had a sense of being pulled in two different directions at the same time. His wife was painfully aware that he was not the same person and also had some concern about his increased drinking at home instead of socialising. Sam's various symptoms amounted to post-traumatic stress disorder (PTSD).

Symptoms of post-traumatic stress disorder

The symptoms of PTSD are detailed in Appendix C and the main features are summarised below under the headings of re-experiencing, avoidance, ruminating, and hyperarousal.

Haunted by memories: re-experiencing

You may feel as if you are drowning in a sea of flashbacks, reminders and nightmares. The umbrella term used to describe these experiences is *intrusions* and it may be that for you they are so vivid that it feels as though the trauma happened yesterday. Less commonly the person can actually lose awareness of their surroundings and for a few minutes feel that the extreme trauma is actually happening now. This is termed a dissociative flashback – those around them are understandably bewildered and disturbed by their strange behaviour. Intrusions are in fact perfectly normal in the weeks and first few months after an extreme trauma; although they are disturbing, they usually fade of their own accord, becoming gradually less frequent and less vivid. However, for about 30 per cent of those experiencing an extreme trauma, disturbing intrusions are still occurring six months or more after the incident and you may have an understandable concern as to whether you will surface from the sea of intrusions.

Unfortunately it is impossible to totally escape reminders of your trauma such as anniversaries or something that triggers the same sights, sounds or smells (a trauma look-alike, e.g. a similar incident on TV). As the anniversaries of your trauma approach the intrusions are likely to increase, rather in the way memories and thoughts of a loved one increase as you get near the anniversary of their death. These anniversary reactions are usually brief and usually reduce further as the years go by. Similarly with the passage of time it will probably become easier for you to distinguish a 'trauma look-alike' from the 'real thing', resulting in less distress at reminders.

'Don't go there': avoidance

You may be avoiding conversations about the incident; if others ask you about it you may at best keep the description to a minimum or simply walk away. This reaction may be based on a belief that if you talk about it you will become upset. You may give a version of the extreme trauma that is rather like a 'police report' of the incident to help minimise distress, leaving out the worst moments of the incident. The 'don't go there' reaction may not be confined to talking about the incident but also apply to the flashback itself. If Sam was at home and had intrusions of his accident, he would have a drink and if at work he would try to busy himself or think of something nice.

Use of an avoidance coping strategy is one of the hall-marks of those struggling in the aftermath of a trauma.

While Sam did not drive at all for three months after the accident because he was too fearful, when he did begin driving he would drive only for 'essential' purposes to and from work, and his family were upset that they no longer had days out.

The escape or avoidance reaction is often also evident in giving up previous hobbies and pastimes and making excuses to avoid contact with others.

Since the accident Sam confined himself to the back kitchen in the evening, while his wife watched TV alone in the lounge. Maria complained that he could go all evening without saying anything and he reluctantly agreed that this was the case.

'Picking' at the memory: ruminating

While you may try to avoid thinking about the incident, you may nevertheless tend to daydream about it.

Sam would not discuss his accident with his wife, but sitting in the back kitchen he found himself dwelling on what would have happened to his children if they had been sitting in the rear of the car when the lorry hit the back. This ruminating would then lead on to remembering the feeling of helplessness he had as he could see in his rear view mirror that a collision was inevitable and the thought 'I will never see my children again'. The focus of the daydreaming would then shift to the chaos caused by his inability to face giving the children a lift in the rear of his car, leaving him feeling demoralised and reaching for the bottle.

The daydreaming represents a relatively undirected thinking and imagining about the trauma (cognition is the technical term used to describe the process of thinking and imagining).

On edge: hyperarousal
You may have a sense of vulnerability or threat persisting even in situations where you know 'objectively' there is no danger.

Sam made a visit to his local pub three months after his accident. Although he was in the company of many friends, he felt he had to sit with the door in view and compelled to inspect all who entered. He did not enjoy the evening, left early and did not return. On his way home, he remembered with embarrassment how he had jumped when a friend dropped a glass ashtray down on the table, and how his friends had laughed. At home Sam would get out of bed a number of times to check that he really had locked the doors and windows and had set his alarm clock. This in turn meant that he had difficulty in getting off to sleep and his sleep was further disturbed by nightmares. His sleeplessness played a part in his irritability.

Preoccupation with the traumatic memory can lead to difficulties in concentration which in turn can affect work performance.

Sam was concerned that his appraisal at work six months after the accident indicated a poor performance. He was especially concerned at this as he knew his firm was downsizing, tried harder to concentrate but was then totally exhausted and very irritable with his family at the end of the working day.

The varying ways in which a traumatised person may be

on edge are covered by the umbrella term disordered arousal or hyperarousal.

Could I be suffering from post-traumatic stress disorder?

To check out whether you may be suffering from PTSD you might want to complete the Trauma Screening Questionnaire (TSQ) in Table 1.1, developed by Professor Chris Brewin and his colleagues (2002) from University College London (reproduced with permission from the *British Journal of Psychiatry*, 2002).

If you have answered six or more with a 'yes' then it is likely, but by no means guaranteed, that you are suffering from PTSD (see Appendices A, B and C for more details).

Kevin completed the TSQ about nine months after he had been assaulted by a group of young men. He endorsed all the items on the TSQ except number 3, but because of National Health Service (NHS) waiting lists, it was a further six months before he saw a psychologist. The psychologist used a structured interview and confirmed that he was indeed suffering from post-traumatic stress disorder. However, the psychologist also noted the extent to which Kevin blamed himself – he had walked alone in a city centre at 2 a.m. to pick up a taxi despite the mild protests of friends he had said goodbye to. The psychologist explained to Kevin that he had trauma-related guilt associated with the PTSD.

Sometimes it comes as a complete surprise to a person to find that they are suffering from PTSD and this may occur after many years of unsuccessful treatment for another disorder.

Angela had suffered from depression all her adult life but it became particularly intense, involving absences from work, after the break up of her marriage. She had had psychological help, but while the therapist was aware of Angela's troubled childhood, physical and mental abuse by her alcoholic mother and sexual abuse by her father, the focus of treatment had been entirely on her maintaining her employment in the local authority and coping with her two children. Angela was troubled by

Table 1.1 Trauma Screening Questionnaire

Your Own Reactions Now to the Traumatic Event

Please consider the following reactions that sometimes occur after a traumatic event. This questionnaire is concerned with your personal reactions to the traumatic event. Please indicate whether or not you have experienced any of the following AT LEAST TWICE IN THE PAST WEEK:

	Yes, at least twice in the past week	No
1 Upsetting thoughts or memories about the event that have come into your mind against your will		
2 Upsetting dreams about the event		
3 Acting or feeling as though the event were happening again		
4 Feeling upset by reminder of the event		
5 Bodily reactions (such as fast heartbeat, stomach churning, sweatiness, dizziness) when reminded of the event		
6 Difficulty falling or staying asleep		
7 Irritability or outbursts of anger		
8 Difficulty concentrating		
9 Heightened awareness of potential danger to yourself and others		
10 Being jumpy or being startled at something unexpected		

Source: Brewin et al. (2002) A brief screening instrument for post-traumatic stress disorder. *British Journal of Psychiatry*, 181: 158–162. Reproduced by permission of The Royal College of Psychiatrists.

flashbacks of trying unsuccessfully to placate her mother, night-mares of her mother entering her room and taking away her two children, and the inappropriate touching of her father, together with avoidance or anything in the media that mentioned abuse. Angela endorsed all but the irritability item on the TSQ: not only was she suffering from PTSD but also she had trauma-related guilt in relation to seeking comfort from her father because he was the only source of any affection. Though Angela was chronically depressed, this was an incomplete description of her difficulties.

What about other disorders?

PTSD is only one of many disorders that you might suffer from following an extreme trauma. Other common problems are phobia, depression, panic disorder and alcohol abuse or dependence. People with a phobia would be distinguished from say someone with PTSD by the presence of predominantly symptoms of escape or avoidance and probably few if any significant re-experiencing symptoms.

Maureen, an elderly lady, was thrown from her seat down the aisle of a bus when it braked sharply. While she had no nightmares or flashbacks of the incident she did develop a phobia of buses and avoided using them if at all possible. In particular she avoided being the sole person getting on a bus.

Some people who are traumatised are not particularly affected by the memory of what happened but much more concerned about what they have become unable to do since the incident, and they may well be suffering from depression. Depression is characterised by persistent low mood (depressed and down most of the day for more than half the days in the month) and a loss of interest and pleasure in things usually enjoyed. It is not simply a matter of being 'fed up' or being 'sad' or 'low': a particular number and combination of symptoms are required (see Appendix C for the diagnostic criteria for depression).

Patrick fell 20 feet from a roof: he had been on a roof ladder which slipped, and his injury to his back meant that afterwards he was unable to do any manual work. He became extremely despondent about this as he had worked all his life as a roofer or on a building site; he felt useless and developed depression.

Some trauma victims develop panic attacks not only in relation to the source of their trauma, e.g. getting in a car, but also unexpectedly, e.g. in a supermarket queue. Repeated unexpected panic attacks are termed panic disorder (see Appendix C for the diagnostic criteria for panic disorder).

Joan was mugged in a city centre and had severe panic attacks whenever she attempted to leave her home. She became house-bound and was diagnosed as suffering from panic disorder with severe agoraphobic avoidance and depression.

Trauma victims can suffer from more than one disorder, for example Sam, who we met at the beginning of this chapter, was by his wife's account abusing alcohol and the professional who saw Sam agreed that he probably did meet diagnostic criteria for alcohol abuse as well as for post-traumatic stress disorder. The more disorders the person is suffering from, the more difficulties they have and treatment has to cover the spectrum of problems.

Additional disorders

Unfortunately if you are suffering from PTSD, there is a good chance you are also suffering from another disorder. For men with PTSD there is a one in two chance of abusing or becoming dependent on alcohol sometime in their life, with a one in three chance of drug abuse or dependence over their lifetime. For women with PTSD the lifetime risk is one in four for both drug abuse or dependence and alcohol abuse or dependence. The abuse of drugs and alcohol is probably best viewed as the PTSD sufferers' attempt to cope with the ongoing sense of vulnerability and threat that is the hallmark of the disorder, but unfortunately substance abuse brings its own complications. Depression is also a common accompaniment of PTSD, with about one in two sufferers having an additional diagnosis of depression. PTSD is often associated with other anxiety disorders. In a study of psychiatric outpatients with PTSD (Brown et al. 2001), 23 per cent met criteria for panic disorder with agoraphobia, 38 per cent for generalised anxiety disorder, 15 per cent for social phobia, 31 per cent for obsessive compulsive disorder and 23 per cent for specific phobia. (For a full description of these additional disorders and their management see Chapter 11.)

Guilt

While guilt is not one of the seventeen PTSD symptoms listed in the American Psychiatric Association's *Diagnostic and Statistical Manual* (2000) or DSM-IV-TR (see Appendix C), the authors of this 'bible' of diagnostic classification have noted that 'individuals with PTSD may describe painful guilt feelings about surviving when others did not survive or about the things they had to do to survive' (American Psychiatric Association 2000: 465); this is termed trauma-related guilt. If the trauma-related guilt persists, it may in turn lead to depression.

Peter saw a colleague fall from three floors up on a building site and was the first to attend to him. Peter could feel that the man's skull was crushed, horrified that he was unrecognisable and alarmed that he did not know what to do. It was a few minutes before the first-aider and the paramedics arrived and they both worked on him for about forty-five minutes before the man died. Peter felt guilty that the man would have had more chance of recovery if he had perhaps held him in a different way or perhaps put him in a different position, as it was he who had cradled him like a baby. He felt too embarrassed to mention this to anyone lest they blame him. Peter suffered from PTSD afterwards but what most debilitated him were his guilt feelings and about three months after the incident, he developed depression.

Pain and emotional disorder

The consequences of an extreme trauma may not be limited to an emotional disorder but physical injuries may result in pain which in some cases becomes chronic. Pain serves to intensify our emotional distress but the reverse is also the case if we get some good news or are in a good mood the pain does not seem as bad. The presence of both PTSD and chronic pain can increase the severity of either condition (Otis et al. 2003). Of those seeking treatment, 20–30 per cent of people with PTSD report chronic pain (Amir et al. 1997; Hubbard et al. 1995). Many people with chronic pain report 'good' and 'bad' days and their emotional state is likely to be influenced by this pattern. An important part of the treatment of trauma victims with chronic pain is teaching them to distinguish the 'better' and the 'worse' ways of handling the pain.

Ian was a bouncer on the door of a club and was shot in the leg, in a case of mistaken identity. His pain acted as a distressing reminder of the incident and he was physically unable to work in this capacity again. He tended to dwell on his inability to work as a bouncer, making it seem that the pain was present for longer and more intensely than it actually was. Ian's pain and PTSD reinforced each other.

To the extent that a person is better able to manage their pain they will be better equipped to manage their emotional problems, be it PTSD, depression, panic disorder or a combination of disorders. It is very unlikely that any psychological strategies will eradicate a long-term pain, but they can stop a trauma victim's life being dictated by the pain, making for a better quality of life.

When there are repeated traumas

People may be traumatised not only by a single event but also by either the same repeated traumas such as physical or sexual abuse in childhood, or assaults by spouse, or multiple traumas arising as part of an occupational role such as police officer, ambulance worker, fire-fighter or soldier. If you have been subjected to repeated or multiple traumas, the various incidents will tend to have merged in your mind, but you will probably be able to recall the worst incident. With this in mind you could complete the TSQ to get an idea as to whether you may be suffering from PTSD. If additional symptoms, such as self-injury, are present, they will often need tackling as well as the PTSD.

Pedro was physically abused by his father from the age of 8 to 11 years. As an adult (despite having a very supportive wife and family) for much of the time he was emotionally numb, unable to have loving feelings for people and coped by stubbing cigarettes out on himself so he could feel something. He could sometimes be embarrassingly moved to tears by an inconsequential sad movie on TV (impaired affect modulation).

A recent trauma can ignite memories of an earlier trauma resulting in more wide-ranging difficulties. Further the debility tends to be greater when the trauma is interpersonal (physical or sexual abuse) as opposed to an accident.

Karen was sexually abused by her cousin (six years her senior) from the age of 8 to 12 years. When aged 11 she took an overdose. At school she felt she did not fit in and was afraid to go places by herself. When she was 18 she began cutting herself at times of stress, but not with the intent of killing herself. Around this time she also took laxatives for several months because she felt she was too fat. Karen had a baby, the baby's father was violent to her and raped her on a number of occasions. She did not disclose the abuse as a child by her cousin until after the rapes. Karen felt that she had always been able to keep the memories of the child abuse in the background until the rapes, after which they had intensified. The psychologist concluded that she had probably been suffering from dysthymic disorder following the sexual abuse, in that she had some symptoms of depression, but fewer than those required for a diagnosis of depression (see Appendix C for the diagnostic criteria for depression) and she had feelings of inadequacy and irritability. A possible alternative diagnosis was borderline personality disorder (key features of borderline personality disorder are an inability to sustain long-term relationships, very abrupt changes in mood and a self-destructive impulsiveness). The psychologist decided against this, however, as Karen was able to relate well to many people long term, including her parents and friends. Indeed, friends thought of Karen as being the life and soul of the party but she felt they could never understand how empty she had always felt inside. Since the rapes, she had been suffering from post-traumatic stress disorder and she berated herself that she had been 'stupid' enough to return to the baby's father after the first rape in response to his and his mother's pleadings, only for history to repeat itself. She had also noticed that since the rapes she had become embarrassed in public situations, for example she could no longer go into a café by herself and have a cup of coffee because she felt all eyes were on her, and at a checkout in a supermarket she hated having to type in her pin number – she was suffering additionally from social phobia.

Brain injury

If you have been rendered unconscious by a trauma, there is a possibility of brain damage: the greater the period of unconsciousness, the greater the likelihood of brain damage. However, great care has to be taken to distinguish symptoms such as poor concentration and lack of motivation that may reflect a depressive response to the trauma from similar symptoms that might arise more directly from an acquired brain injury. To complicate matters even further, depression and brain injury can coexist. It is really a matter for a neuro-psychologist or neurologist to decide whether and to what extent there is brain injury. People with mild brain injuries may continue to hold down jobs, even quite responsible jobs, but they may have difficulties in organising or planning work (executive functioning), putting themselves in other people's shoes (empathy), in the speed of information processing and in retaining and operating on what they have been told. However, if they were exceptionally competent before the trauma, it may not be apparent that their current functioning at work and home represents a poorer performance.

Sandra was a lawyer. While climbing with her partner Colin in Wales, they fell a few hundred feet, she landed on top of him and he was killed. Fortunately, there were other climbers nearby who summoned help. Sandra was airlifted to hospital and was unconscious for several hours. Despite her injuries she attended Colin's funeral a week later. Others remarked how well she seemed to be coping, and then they observed that she had always been a 'coper'. Within a few months she returned to jogging, albeit on the flat as opposed to over hills. She went back to work but noticed that after coming out of meetings with partners, she felt lost, unsure what had been decided and what should be done. At home she no longer initiated conversations with her mother and was much less physically demonstrative with relatives. She had also lost her sense of smell. Initially she attributed her difficulties to a bereavement reaction but the symptoms persisted and twelve months afterwards, at the prompting of a colleague specialising in compensation claims, an appointment was made for her to attend a neuropsychologist. The neuropsychological tests were conducted over two meetings and in the subsequent report it was concluded that she was not taking in new information quite as quickly as she likely would have done before her fall, nor was she able to plan and organise herself as well as she likely did beforehand. The neuropsychologist summarised her new-found difficulties by describing her as having mild cognitive impairment and recommended cognitive behavioural therapy (CBT).

Learning difficulties

A trauma victim who also has learning difficulties is especially disadvantaged and will likely find it impossible to directly utilise self-help books or standard therapy. However, if you are a carer or family member of a trauma survivor with mild learning difficulties (IQ in the range 55 to 70), you can support them by using the visual aids in Chapter 2 (Figures 2.1, 2.2 and 2.3) to effectively communicate what has gone wrong with them since the trauma. You can also help them by teaching very practical strategies such as 'Stop-Think-Relax' (described in Chapter 8). For those with moderate learning difficulties, the carers or family may have to regularly go over the meaning of the visual prompts and conduct more rehearsals of strategies. For those with severe learning difficulties, there is no reason to suppose that they are not as devastated as others by extreme trauma. However, help proffered would have to be primarily non-verbal, e.g. hugs, music, no-hands massage (a powerful form of massage that avoids injury to the masseur's hands). In this way those with profound learning difficulties may regain a sense of safety and trust.

The response of people with learning difficulties to extreme trauma is as varied as anyone else's.

Jack had mild learning difficulties and had just stepped out from behind the bus that dropped him off at home from his day centre when he was hit by a car. His mother heard a commotion outside her home and found Jack lying in the road and very agitated. Jack was taken to hospital but his physical injuries were not that serious and he was discharged home a few hours later. Following the accident he became very lethargic and anxious, e.g. refusing to attend his weekly swimming class or to stay at his sister's overnight. He lost his confidence to walk by himself to his local shop because it would mean crossing a side road. Jack became verbally abusive to his mother and sister and was threatened with expulsion from his day centre because of his disruptive behaviour. Jack had some symptoms of anxiety and some of depression but insufficient for either condition alone; he met diagnostic criteria for 'anxiety disorder not otherwise specified'.

How traumatic does a traumatic event have to be?

The DSM-IV-TR (2000) lists a very wide range of events that may lead to PTSD, some of them (e.g. victim of a serious road traffic accident, bombing or natural disaster) are more obvious than others (e.g. childbirth, suffering from cancer). Sometimes it is debatable as to whether a particular event actually qualifies.

Emma was six months pregnant when she stepped out of a taxi into a pothole and had a nasty fall. She was very anxious about her unborn child, particularly because she had had two previous miscarriages and she had become depressed after the last one. At hospital after her fall the staff reassured her that the baby was fine but she had nightmares of getting out of the taxi and miscarrying. This and her other 'PTSD' symptoms continued until after the baby was born. It is debatable whether a 'fall in pregnancy' should be put in the same category as the other extreme traumas. A few weeks after the birth of her baby, Emma developed panic attacks and became fearful of going out of her neighbourhood by

Dedicated to Isaac, born 7 July 2005 – the day of the London bombings.

No horror has the last word.

herself. She was diagnosed by her general practitioner (GP) as having panic disorder with moderate agoraphobic avoidance.

While Emma's case is at the border of the type of trauma that might lead to PTSD, some traumas such as non-physical bullying at work would not be considered extreme enough. Scott and Stradling (1994) have however described cases where patients have met the symptom criteria for PTSD, i.e. with significant symptoms under all the cluster headings B, C and D in Appendix C, but from events such as bullying at work or caring for a relative with a progressive neurological illness. Scott and Stradling (1994) termed this prolonged duress stress disorder (PDSD). Further they suggested that from a clinical point of view the PDSD patients should be treated as if they were suffering from PTSD. (It remains to be demonstrated whether the neurobiology of PDSD and PTSD are distinct: the evidence so far suggests great similarity but a slight difference.)

Bob developed PTSD-like symptoms (PDSD) after a year of working under a boss who cursed him whenever he failed to solve a problem, and whose reply was 'Don't give me problems, just solutions' whenever Bob tried to explain himself or ask for more resources. He had nightmares of being humiliated in front of colleagues and felt nauseous when he approached work. Further his concentration worsened and this attracted more criticism from his boss. At home he had become uncharacteristically irritable and was avoiding socialising.

Children and adolescents

Children and adolescents often display their post-trauma reactions in different ways from adults. DSM-IV-TR (2000) notes (see Appendix C) that at the time of the trauma the young person's response may involve disorganised or agitated behaviour rather than the more adult response of intense, fear, helplessness or horror. Further, young children may re-enact the traumatic incident in play. Children may show their distress by bed-wetting, sleepwalking or developmental regression, e.g. going back to thumb-sucking or biting finger nails.

Like traumatised adults, children may avoid talking about their trauma and this may give parents and teachers a false sense of relief that they are not affected. However, it is also possible that the child who does not talk about it may not be affected at all or only marginally. In gauging the impact of a trauma on a child, account needs to be taken of any deterioration in their schoolwork and their relationships. Matters can be complicated when a parent is also involved in the same trauma as the child.

Cecilia was driving her car, with her three children, Anthony aged 3, Abigail aged 6 and Amanda aged 14, as passengers, on a motorway when she had a blowout. The car veered across the motorway, narrowly missing a bridge and coming to rest on the hard shoulder. On clinical examination Cecilia and Abigail were found to be suffering from PTSD, while Anthony had become very clingy. Cecilia was insistent that Amanda was as badly affected as herself, but on examination her older daughter was found to be slightly anxious as a passenger, more so if her mother was driving, but her functioning was not so impaired that she was regarded as having a phobia. Amanda was more irritable since the accident, however, and reacted to her mother's increased irritability; she also had difficulties concentrating in school (her grades became Ds rather than As). For about three months after the accident Amanda wet her bed at night and borrowed Anthony's dummies for use each night (developmental regression) but had only occasionally used them since. Even though her parents would assure her that they had locked the house up at night, she would feel compelled to get out of bed and check that everything was locked and appliances were switched off. Though her checking behaviour was reminiscent of obsessive compulsive disorder it did not go on for hours and as such she did not meet DSM criteria for OCD. The accident had left Amanda with a slight scar on her right cheekbone and she was very self-conscious about this, insisting on not going out without a lot of make-up on and avoiding swimming and sports. Cecilia told Amanda that she was overreacting but she was adamant that the scar made her ugly. Amanda was suffering from body dysmorphic disorder, an exaggerated concern about a minor physical anomaly. In a sense Cecilia was correct that Amanda's overall impairment in functioning was much the same as her own but the presentation was different, post-traumatic stress disorder and body dysmorphic disorder respectively.

Just as the assessment of traumatised children is somewhat different from that of adults so too are the effective coping strategies. The difficulties of children are addressed in Chapter 12.

A thumbnail sketch

A thumbnail sketch of your worst trauma and its effects can act as a passport to others including friends, family doctor or counsellor beginning to understand where you are coming from. Table 1.2 can be used for this purpose.

If you complete a sentence or two about each of the five parts of Table 1.2, it will put others in the picture and summarise matters for yourself. Additionally if you complete the Trauma Screening Questionnaire (Table 1.1 on page 10) and also hand it to your doctor or counsellor, it is a very useful starting point for them. Some people might not be able to put in writing the completed sentences, but a friend or family member or professional can do the writing if someone asks the first part. Alternatively children can be asked to draw anything scary that pops into their mind during the day or at night, or say anything they do not want to do now, or describe anything they keep thinking of and describe the worst part of what happened. The adults can write down any comments the children make about their pictures. However,

Table 1.2 **Thumbnail sketch of your worst trauma**

1 I have flashbacks/nightmares of ....
2 I avoid..
3 I keep thinking ....
4 Being on edge has affected ....
5 The worst part of what happened was ....

adults have to be very careful not to lead or suggest to the child what they draw as this will give a very misleading impression as to what really bothers them. Sometimes adults cannot bear to complete the 'worst part of what happened was ...', it feels too painful and in writing it down it makes it too real. But it is a help anyway to complete whatever part of Table 1.2 you can as it is an important first step.

In completing Table 1.2 you are spelling out the problem. Many problems are not solved, not because they are too difficult but because they are not clearly spelled out: they are fuzzy or vague.

Cecilia complained that her daughter had an 'attitude' problem since the accident but her husband insisted that she was just a typical teenager who was a little more fearful than previously in a car. His tighter definition of the situation offered greater hope than Cecilia's.

To ensure that you are giving a comprehensive picture of the trauma and its effects, it is important to make a note of any coping strategies such as drinking more alcohol. You should also note the extent to which you believe pain is interfering with your life.

Moving on

Using the framework of Table 1.2, John, who was involved in a gas explosion at work, wrote:

> I keep having *nightmares* of the ball of fire coming towards me but it is as if it is in slow motion. I *avoid* the place where I worked. Even switching the cooker on at home, I keep *thinking* I shouldn't be here. Seconds earlier and I would not have been. The *worst* part was seeing Alan on fire and my struggling to put out his flames with my hands. My sleep and concentration have been badly *affected*. I hate to say it but I *drink* more so that I can get off to sleep and my partner complains about it. My physical injuries are nothing compared to Alan's and I shouldn't complain about the little *pain* I have, but I do.

In completing Table 1.2 John has in effect written a chapter in

his autobiography – he was later diagnosed as suffering from PTSD.

The danger for trauma victims is that this 'chapter' of their autobiography becomes the only one that counts. Previous chapters about how they viewed themselves, others and life itself can be dismissed as having no significance. In chapters following the trauma and its effects, the victim has to move on, invest in life again and create a story that does justice not only to the trauma but also to the view of life pre-trauma. Clearly those whose life before the worst trauma was pretty traumatic are at more of a disadvantage in putting their 'nightmare' in a wider context.

Tessa went riding on holiday, the horse bolted and she was thrown from the horse. She sustained a head injury and was unconscious for several hours. She severely damaged her leg and eighteen months later was still able to walk only with the help of crutches. She was in considerable pain: amputation had been considered but in her case there was no guarantee this would relieve the pain. Tessa became depressed and was embarrassed at the scarring on her forehead. She ensured that she always wore a hat and kept her hair over her scar. Her husband, Bill, and close friends protested that the scar was hardly noticeable but she dismissed their challenge with a sharp 'I can see it'. Tessa particularly avoided going out in the wind and the rain, fearing exposure of her scar. She was suffering from body dysmorphic disorder, an exaggerated concern about a minor or imagined physical anomaly with regard to the scar. Tessa also found that she was losing track of films on TV and had to get others to explain them at the end. She would feel sure she had done things when she had not and had to use lists constantly. A neuropsychological examination revealed mild cognitive impairment.

Summary of the characters introduced in this chapter

We shall meet the characters introduced in this chapter at various points throughout the book to illustrate just how they can be helped to move on. The cast comprises:

1 Sam – probable PTSD following road traffic accident and drink problem
2 Kevin – PTSD and trauma-related guilt after being assaulted
3 Angela – depression and post-traumatic stress disorder following physical and sexual abuse in childhood and adolescence
4 Maureen – phobia about getting on a bus and generalised anxiety disorder
5 Patrick – depression after falling off a roof
6 Joan – panic disorder and severe agoraphobic avoidance and depression after being mugged
7 Peter – trauma-related guilt, PTSD, depression after trying to help man who fell from scaffolding
8 Ian – shot at work, pain a major problem as well as PTSD
9 Pedro – physically abused from aged 8 to 11, PTSD and associated symptoms of PTSD and depression
10 Karen – PTSD and social phobia following rape and dysthymic disorder following childhood sexual abuse
11 Sandra – mild brain injury following a climbing accident
12 Jack – already existing mild learning difficulties and anxiety disorder not otherwise specified after a pedestrian road traffic accident
13 Emma – possible PTSD after tripping while pregnant after getting out of taxi and later panic disorder with moderate agoraphobic avoidance
14 Bob – prolonged duress stress disorder after bullying at work
15 Cecilia – PTSD and obsessive compulsive disorder after road traffic accident
16 Amanda – 14-year-old girl suffering from body dysmorphic disorder.
17 Abigail – 6-year-old girl with post-traumatic stress disorder
18 Anthony – 3-year-old boy with traumatic stress reaction
19 John – PTSD and depression as a result of a gas explosion at work
20 Tessa – body dysmorphic disorder, mild brain injury, pain and depression since riding accident.

2

Making sense of my reactions

While it may be comforting to know that there is a particular label or diagnosis for your difficulties, you may nevertheless be speechless at some of your reactions, mentally beating yourself up.

Cecilia was insistent that her 14-year-old daughter, Amanda, retrieve her muddy shoes from behind the front door immediately and go and clean them. Amanda protested that there was no immediate need to do so as she had only just arrived home. An argument ensued. Just then her father, Dave, arrived home and complained that he did not need to be greeted by 'mayhem' after a hard day at work. Cecilia went off and sulked. It was 2–3 hours before she acknowledged that there had been no reason to ask Amanda in the first place to clean her muddy shoes. Feeling guilty, she went and apologised, but unfortunately Amanda declared that she had 'had enough', and did not want to hear any more. Cecilia then relayed this to her husband, Dave, who was not very sympathetic and blamed her that no evening meal had been cooked because of her sulk. At this, Cecilia went for a walk, bewildered about what was happening to her and her family since the accident.

The 'dodgy alarm'

On her walk Cecilia reflected that since the accident she overreacted to anything that was not exactly as it should be and to any reminders of the incident but later on her reactions appeared totally stupid. But to make matters worse, knowing they were 'stupid' did not seem to prevent her doing the same again and she felt out of control. Later in counselling Cecilia was much relieved to be given a 'map' of her difficulties and the map itself suggested ways out of her problems. A key 'site' on the trauma map is the brain's alarm, the amygdala. It was explained to Cecilia that before her accident, it was as if the setting of her alarm indicated a place of safety, and now it was as if the accident had knocked the alarm and she was in a war zone (see Figure 2.1).

It was explained to Cecilia that in a war zone, one would want everything to be just so; there would be little tolerance of anything not going to plan. Further travelling as a passenger in a car, now with her husband Dave driving, she would be in a war zone issuing instructions to watch for various 'dangers' while he would be simply motoring in a safe place, perplexed at her reactions. Essentially Cecilia was on permanent sentry duty and this resulted in interference with her sleep and concentration. Her alarm was set so sensitively that it would go off now at any unexpected noise or movement or the slightest irritation.

The amygdala is not simply an alarm: it is also thought to be the site of emotional memory and it remembers the sights, sounds and smells involved in the trauma (see LeDoux 1998). This in turn results in intrusive images of the trauma sometimes occurring for no apparent reason and at other times

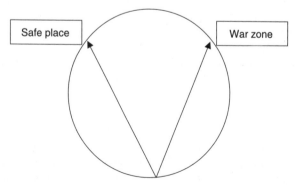

Figure 2.1 **The brain's alarm: the amygdala.**

cued by reminders. The amygdala does not operate using language or logic, it works on a matching.

Whenever Cecilia came across reminders of the accident, she automatically felt intense fear. The amygdala, although situated in the brain, has connections to the top of the stomach and whenever Cecilia saw bridges over motorways, she experienced a wave of fear rising from the top of her stomach, accompanied by sweating and palpitations. Sitting at home she knew perfectly well that she was safe on a motorway with her husband driving, as she acknowledged that in fact Dave as an advanced police driver was safer than her, but this knowledge did not seem to make any difference when they were travelling together – to her frustration and Dave's chagrin.

The amygdala operates at both a conscious and a non-conscious level so that a person suffering from PTSD will not necessarily know what triggered an intense recollection of the incident or why they should have had a nightmare of their trauma on a particular night. Panic disorder is a common accompaniment of post-traumatic stress disorder and in both disorders the amygdala plays an important role. While in PTSD the amygdala is responding to an extreme external stressor, in panic disorder it is reacting to unusual but not abnormal bodily sensations. For example a person with both disorders might run up stairs at home focusing on what they were looking for. The consequent heart racing might be sufficient to trip the hypersensitive alarm resulting in a full-blown panic attack.

The bubble

Those suffering from PTSD tend to live their life in a 'bubble' (see Figure 2.2), feeling cut off from others. This is typified by Cecilia going for a walk by herself, pondering her over-the-top reaction to her daughter and inability to communicate with her husband.

The sufferer is aware that they are not connecting with others as they would before the trauma. Typically telephone calls are not returned, excuses are made to get out of social engagements and visits to friends or family are curtailed.

Figure 2.2 **The bubble.**

The person with PTSD is haunted by a sense of vulnerability or threat (biologically it is as if they are in a 'war zone') that is not shared by friends, family or colleagues, resulting in intense feelings of isolation. For many suffering PTSD the only 'safe place' they believe is home, despite a tense atmosphere there created by poor communication. When they are out of the home, they want to be back as soon as possible, but if visitors come they are looking at their watch waiting for them to go! Over time the PTSD sufferer becomes aware that home has all the 'safety' of a prison cell or bunker and they can become increasingly depressed.

Emotional flatness

It has often been observed that injured soldiers on battle-fields have managed to get themselves to sources of help many miles away and only there do they feel the full pain of their injuries. In these extreme situations it seems that the body's natural opioids kick in, acting as an analgesic, permitting the victim to reach safety. While this is a useful mechanism at the time of the trauma, it seems that in chronic PTSD, the excess production of opioids has not been switched off, resulting in an emotional numbness. Many PTSD sufferers are embarrassed that they no longer have loving feelings for their children or passion for their partner. To make matters worse, they may misattribute emotional numbness to deficiencies in their children or partner or themselves. It is as if someone has left the top off a lemonade bottle and the 'fizz' has gone (see Figure 2.3).

Threat evaluation system: the amygdala and hippocampus

The amygdala does not single-handedly evaluate threat; it interacts with another part of the brain, the hippocampus, which locates events in time and place.

Thus Cecilia could press the hippocampus into service by telling herself that the blowout in the car on the motorway was a one-off in that she had travelled thousands of times on it without any disaster and probably would do so in the future.

In this way the hippocampus can attempt to rein in the amygdala, preventing an amygdala hijack. The hippocampus is connected to the long-term memory store and is in effect responsible for writing the story of the trauma, updating it as new perspectives suggest themselves.

For example Cecilia's story was initially focused on her feelings of helplessness as her car veered across the motorway. Later however she focused on the fact that she had managed to stop on the hard shoulder rather than go down an embankment.

Both the amygdala and hippocampus act via the hypothalamic pituitary axis releasing stress hormones into the bloodstream. The effect of the amygdala is to increase readiness

Figure 2.3 **Emotional flatness.**

for fight or flight while the hippocampus exerts a soothing effect. Ideally the amygdala and hippocampus strike a balance that is appropriate for the situation the person is in at the time. One way of understanding the interplay between the amygdala and the hippocampus is of thinking that the former creates a stream of red paint while the latter issues forth white paint (see Figure 2.4) and the right balance (of stress hormones) for the body is the colour pink.

Unfortunately Cecilia appears to have been hijacked by the amygdala and is coloured white. Prior to her accident Cecilia believed that if she just took a bit of care in life and was 'sensible', then all would be well. It was as if her hormone system was 'reddish' rather than pink, dominated by her hippocampus. Now, however, the hippocampus hardly gets a look in.

There are two ways of trying to achieve the desirable 'pink' state: one is to reduce the output from the amygdala (white) and the other is to increase the output from hippocampus (red). Treatments for post-traumatic stress disorder have aspects such as gradual exposure to what is feared that effect the output from the amygdala and other features such as realistic thinking (cognitive restructuring) that target the hippocampus.

The threat evaluation and control-demand systems

The threat evaluation system does not necessarily have the last word: it is affected by the brain's control-demand system,

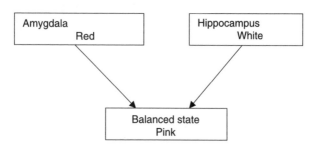

Figure 2.4 **Achieving an appropriate balance of stress hormones.**

which is focused on getting tasks done in the here and now. In principle the control-demand system could override a threat evaluation system. The two key players in the control-demand system are the anterior cingulate and the dorsolateral prefrontal cortex.

Cecilia could decide, despite her PTSD, to read each night storybooks to her younger daughter Abigail and son Anthony, disregarding her emotional numbness and fearing the approach of the night and the inevitable nightmares.

What am I like?

Which character's reactions so far best match your own? The characters are composite cases of people whom I have treated, and disguised to protect their identity. Throughout this book there are suggestions as to how each of them might move forward.

How well do the 'dodgy alarm', 'bubble' and 'lemonade bottle without a top' fit you?

To get an accurate model of how you operate, ask yourself the following set of questions. You might also get someone close to you to answer the same set of questions. Many people who have been traumatised are so preoccupied with their own thoughts and feelings that it comes as a surprise to find out how others see them.

1 How 'alarmed' are you or do you seem to others?

How vulnerable or threatened do you feel? Perhaps, in the immediate aftermath of the extreme trauma, you felt as if you were indeed in a war zone, but now it is more like being in a risky neighbourhood. On the spectrum 'safe place' to 'war zone', where would you place yourself now? Knowing where your alarm is set makes it easier to understand how much of your current reaction is in fact background emotion to the trauma and how much truly belongs to the events of today.

2 To what extent are you isolating yourself?

Do you still confide in those close to you? Do you contact friends or family much less? How much are you investing in others since the trauma? What would be the best investment policy long term with regard to others? Do others see you isolating yourself?

3 How emotionally flat or numb do you feel or seem to others?

How much of the time do you feel empty or flat? How much of a problem is this? Does this lack of feeling affect what you do, such as hugging. Do you feel guilty over your lack of feelings?

4 Have you been hijacked by the amygdala?

How would you have described the balance between your thinking and feeling before your trauma? Did your heart tend to rule your head or the other way around? Perhaps you had them nicely in balance? Does your thinking now tend to be totally at odds with your feelings? Nowadays do you ever do an override of your feelings knowing that what you do will be in your own or other long-tem interests? Is it as if you have a notice up that says 'feelings rule OK', and so you indulge more in alcohol? Ask someone close to also answer this series of questions in relation to you.

What fuels the PTSD?

Negative beliefs in relation to each of the symptoms that may comprise a post-traumatic response help fuel the persistence of debility.

Sam took his re-experiencing of flashbacks of his accident as meaning 'something bad is going to happen any time' and that therefore avoidance of driving when possible was important, thus avoidance was justified. He believed it was right to be on sentry duty (hyperarousal) even to the extent of stopping his young children climbing on the furniture and he was cross with himself for his lack of warmth (emotional numbing) to his wife.

PTSD also persists because the story of the trauma has not been updated and a new story developed to compete with the old, so that it is this revised memory that is accessed in preference to the original version of events. Unfortunately traumatic memories cannot be erased, they are not like a memory on the hard drive of a computer, but a more adaptive memory can be constructed which can then compete with the old and in effect override it. (The ability of this new memory to achieve an override can be negated by the use of alcohol or drugs.) The new adaptive memory is such that in effect the hippocampus and amygdala are working in synchrony and the output from the threat evaluation system does not sabotage the operation of the control demand system.

Sam was stuck with the memory of looking in his rear view mirror, seeing the lorry approach at speed and thinking he would never see his children again. An updated version would be acknowledging this memory when it occurs, while simultaneously looking at a picture of his children or playing with them as a reminder that, contrary to predictions, he did survive.

3

Will I get better?

Probably you will get better, but some traumas are more debilitating than others and have a reduced likelihood of recovery. In a study of rape victims, Rothbaum et al. (1992) found that 64 per cent were suffering from PTSD four weeks after the trauma. This proportion reduced to 47 per cent after three months and to 42 per cent by six months. A similar study (Rothbaum and Foa 1993) conducted on assault victims found a smaller proportion to have been traumatised: 14.6 per cent had PTSD three months following the trauma and at six months the proportion was 11.5 per cent. In a study of road traffic accident victims, Blanchard and Hickling (1997) found that about half those who did develop PTSD recovered by a six-month follow-up. Thereafter very few people improved. (On the basis of these studies one would say that the prospects of recovery are better for Cecilia (road traffic accident victim) than for Karen (rape victim), both of whom we met in Chapter 1.) In a study of fire-fighters who attended a bush fire in Australia, McFarlane (1988) assessed subjects at four months, eleven months and twenty-nine months after the incident. At first assessment 30.2 per cent developed PTSD and approximately one-half of these (47.4 per cent) had remitted seven months later, a further 18.9 per cent had remitted by twenty-nine months, leaving one in three of those who originally developed PTSD with persistent chronic PTSD. A further 19.7 per cent developed PTSD after the initial assessment. Similarly in a study by Blanchard and Hickling (1997) of those with some but not a full set of PTSD symptoms (sub-syndromal PTSD) 15 per cent of them later went on to develop full PTSD. Thus, not having full PTSD in the immediate aftermath of a trauma is not an absolute guarantee that the person will not succumb to it, but it is unlikely. Overall it is possible to conclude that a significant minority of those who suffer PTSD continued to be debilitated in the long term and that the proportion varies with the type of trauma.

What makes a difference?

Blanchard and Hickling (1997) illuminate the factors in the recovery process. Using a structured interview these authors reassessed road traffic accident victims six and twelve months after an initial assessment conducted between one and four months post trauma. The factors in Table 3.1 were found to be predictive of either their diagnostic status or severity of PTSD on at least one follow-up point. The more severe any one of the predictors, the less chance of recovery, e.g. the more severe the initial PTSD the less chance of recovery, the more severely physically injured the less chance of recovery, and so on.

Looking at Table 3.1 the prospects of recovery for Cecilia are better than for Sam, though they both had PTSD following their accidents. Sam had also been abusing alcohol.

Brewin et al. (2000) reviewed a large number of studies

Table 3.1 **Predictors of recovery at least one follow-up point**

1 Initial severity of PTSD symptoms
2 Physical injury
3 Past or present alcohol abuse
4 Past or present major depression
5 Pre-accident personality disorder
6 Irritability
7 A sense of a foreshortened future
8 New family trauma
9 Post trauma family relations
10 Vulnerability in car at time of assessment.

Source: based on Blanchard and Hickling 1997

involving a wide range of trauma. Unsurprisingly they found that the more severe the trauma, the more likely the person was to develop PTSD. In keeping with this Maureen, who you may remember was thrown out of her seat on a bus, developed a phobia about getting on a bus and generalised anxiety disorder, while Karen developed PTSD following her rapes, and Ian had PTSD following the shooting. What was surprising about Brewin's study was that it was events that happened after the trauma, lack of social support and additional life stress that more strongly predicted the development of PTSD, rather than events before, such as having been abused as a child or a previous psychiatric history. The biggest single predictor was lack of social support following the trauma. In particular it was the negative social interactions aspect of 'lack of social support' rather than the absence of positive support that most predicted the development of PTSD.

Going with the grain of the recovery process

As negative social interactions in the wake of a trauma dispose a person to suffer from PTSD, it is appropriate to seek to reduce them. In reading this book you might be able to better communicate about your distress with those closest to you, thereby reducing negative social interactions, and you may have in effect taken the first step in resolving your post trauma symptoms. Similarly if your counsellor has engaged your partner or friend in the counselling process, this can help to build bridges between you and ultimately reduce symptoms. Extreme traumas do throw up additional life stresses, such as financial problems arising from an inability to work. Such additional stresses are second in importance only to lack of social support in disposing a person to suffer from PTSD. Consequently the better these stresses are managed, the less the likelihood of developing PTSD.

Previous problems

If you were abused as a child and then, as an adult, experience an extreme trauma, it is likely to make you think more about your earlier experiences. The recent trauma may create an emotional state similar to that in your abusive childhood; in those circumstances you are likely to have more frequent and vivid recall of the early trauma. You may therefore also have to learn afresh how to handle these old memories as well as the newer horror. There is likely to be more work for you to do than for other trauma victims without the disturbing earlier memories, but you can still move forward. Unfortunately it is likely that if you were abused as a child, your amygdala was sensitised, so that you were more likely to develop a faulty alarm in the wake of a trauma.

Approximately one-quarter of the population suffer from anxiety or depression or some other emotional disorder at some point in their life, and they are more likely to be debilitated following an extreme trauma. Further it is likely that what they suffered previously, such as depression or panic disorder, will be resurrected. If you had a previous psychiatric history the previous difficulties will probably also need to be tackled as well as the post trauma response.

Additional problems

If you are suffering from PTSD the likelihood is that you are suffering from at least one other disorder as well. Breslau and his colleagues (1991) found that 83 per cent of individuals with PTSD met criteria for one or more other disorders. The most common co-morbid conditions include depression, substance abuse and other anxiety disorders. The more additional disorders you have, the more difficulty you are likely to have in recovering.

A psychosis is a severe mental disorder in which the person may suffer from delusions, e.g. that they are an alien, and/or hallucinations in which they see, smell, feel, taste or hear things that others do not. Psychosis is much rarer than anxiety or depressive disorders, but there is evidence that trauma can play a causal role in the development of psychosis. In a study by Mueser and colleagues (1998) 37 per cent of those with a diagnosis of schizoaffective disorder and 28 per cent of those with a diagnosis of schizophrenia also met the DSM criteria for PTSD, whereas in the general population the lifetime risk of PTSD is less than 9 per cent. A history of physical or sexual abuse is unusually common in psychotic women, with between 51 and 97 per cent of women reporting some form of physical or sexual abuse in their lifetime. There is usually a time gap between the trauma and the psychosis and the precise mechanism by which one can lead to the other is not yet understood. However, Scott and Stradling (1994) have presented case examples of PTSD symptoms arising from cumulative stressors without the direct experience of acute precipitating trauma. It is possible therefore that prolonged duress can in some individuals lead to both PTSD and psychosis and that this occurs with a progressive sensitisation of the amygdala.

4

What works?

Of those who complete treatment for PTSD with various forms of cognitive behavioural therapy (CBT) or eye movement desensitisation and reprocessing (EMDR), more than half improve. Looking at those who complete treatment, 67 per cent no longer meet criteria for PTSD, and of those who enter treatment (whether or not they complete), the recovery rate is 56 per cent (Bradley et al. 2005). However, the clinical trials for PTSD have excluded roughly 30 per cent patients referred for treatment and those studies with more exclusion criteria have produced better results. There is thus a concern about the extent to which one can generalise from the outcome studies to individuals in the community with PTSD who may also have a number of additional disorders. Nevertheless both CBT and EMDR are clearly helpful to at least half of PTSD sufferers.

CBT is the most researched and well validated of treatments for a range of emotional disorders. The effectiveness of a treatment can be gauged by a metric, called *effect size*, which compares how well the average patient does in the treatment group with how well the average person does in a comparison control group (e.g. waiting list group). Butler et al. (2006) found large effect sizes for depression, generalised anxiety disorder, panic disorder, social phobia, PTSD and childhood depressive and anxiety disorders. Moderate effect sizes were found for marital distress, anger, childhood somatic disorders and chronic pain. Further CBT was somewhat superior to antidepressants in the treatment of adult depression.

What is CBT?

CBT is based on the idea that how you think plays an important part in how you feel. For example, if a colleague fails to greet you one morning, you might think 'He's an ignorant sod' or alternatively 'He's in a world of his own, not surprising given all that is going on at home'. The former would produce anger and the latter sympathy. The essence of CBT is checking out whether a first negative interpretation is valid or in need of some modification. The other major component of CBT focuses on behaviour, in particular using behavioural experiments to test out negative predictions.

Cecilia decided to test out her belief that she could never drive on motorways again, by driving just one junction on a Sunday morning, and discovered that it was not as bad as she thought.

In CBT clients are taught cognitive (thoughts and images) and behavioural strategies to manage their difficulties. Different types of thinking are prominent in different disorders and so the focus of treatment is also different.

Joan, who was suffering from panic disorder following her assault, had catastrophic thoughts about any bodily sensations when she left her home, such as 'My heart is racing, I am going to have a heart attack'.

Kevin, who was suffering from PTSD following his assault, interpreted his irritability to mean that his personality had changed for the worse. He also interpreted his emotional numbing to mean that he would never be able to relate to others again and he interpreted his flashbacks to mean that he was going mad.

Studies have shown (Dunmore et al. 1999, 2001) that people who early on report negative interpretations of symptoms are slower to recover from PTSD. CBT treatments differ for different disorders because, as the founding father of cognitive therapy Aaron Beck put it, they differ in their cognitive content (Alford and Beck 1997).

CBT also addresses how people cope with their difficulties. For example, Joan coped with her panic attacks by not going out so as to avoid them, but this left her more exposed to her hypercritical husband. Kevin blocked thoughts and images (cognitions) of his assault by getting up from where he was seated and busying himself. Sam behaved similarly to the flashbacks of his accident but would additionally 'soothe' himself with alcohol. CBT seeks to eliminate the cognitive (e.g. Kevin and Sam) and behavioural (e.g. Joan) avoidance.

Studies have shown that avoidance and thought suppression are related to slower recovery from PTSD (Dunmore et al. 1999, 2001). While it does seem commonsense to try not to think of what upsets you unfortunately it does not actually work. Try for a moment *not* to think about 'PINK ELEPHANTS'. In trying not to think about them you think of them more in the end – a rebound effect.

There are in fact various forms of CBT for PTSD, including cognitive processing therapy (Resick and Schnicke 1993), exposure therapy (Foa and Rothbaum 1998), metacognitive therapy (Wells and Sembi 2004) and cognitive contextual therapy (Scott and Stradling 2006). My own cognitive contextual therapy not only incorporates cognitive and behavioural strategies but also places a special emphasis on the role that relationships can play in the resolution of symptoms. Additionally cognitive contextual therapy recognises that sometimes the best way to change an emotion is to replace it with another emotion.

Bob, who had been bullied at work and had prolonged duress stress disorder, could in principle replace his feelings of sadness and demoralisation with anger at his employer.

What is the format of CBT treatment sessions?

CBT is primarily about learning new skills with which to tackle problems that bother you. As such it is primarily educational and the therapist is principally an educator. It is similar to counselling in that it is essential that the therapist shows an understanding of how you feel (empathy), warmth and genuineness. Although these qualities are necessary for any teacher, they are not by themselves sufficient for you to learn the skills of handling your problems better. The teacher also needs some technical knowledge of how the disorder comes about and what strategies have been found to work and what have not. Thus CBT is very different from general counselling. Comparisons of CBT and support-ive counselling have consistently shown that the former is superior to the latter (e.g. see Resick and Schnicke 1993). If you have been put off by your experience of counselling, do not let this deter you from seeking CBT: it really is different.

CBT begins by the therapist listening to your story of the trauma and its effects. The therapist then shares with you a map of your difficulties, by for example using the diagrams in Chapter 2, and applying them to your par-ticular experiences. The therapist then teaches some skills, for example how to practise a *detached mindfulness* when flashbacks of the incident occur rather than blocking it.

At the next session the therapist reviews how you got on with your detached mindfulness homework and will help you refine your technique if you had difficulties. Then further strategies are taught and included in the homework assign-ment. The therapist does not dominate the sessions, however. You are asked if there are any particular concerns that you want to put onto the agenda and time is allocated to discuss these. Thus you might want to bring up, say, your loss of libido since the trauma and some discussion might take place of the extent to which it is a direct consequence of the trauma and how much it might be a side-effect of the anti-depressant medication that you might be taking. This then leads to the distillation of a way forward with regard to the sexual difficulties.

The therapist in CBT is rather like a driving instructor, who is important because he or she teaches new skills, but is reliant on you to practise, practise and practise. It is you who puts in the spadework and you who suffers the inevitable two steps forward and one step back as you progress through therapy. In learning any new skill, setbacks are par for the course but if they are budgeted for, you still move on, learning from the mistakes.

CBT is a structured approach to emotional difficulties but not in a rigid and inflexible way. Typically for PTSD or depression, about twelve treatment sessions are scheduled, while for a phobia it would probably be about eight sessions. However, the number of sessions is likely to be greater if there are additional disorders such as alcohol abuse. The first sessions are usually weekly, with larger gaps as therapy progresses. Treatment is usually completed within six months.

The self-help material in this book can usefully complement a CBT treatment programme. NHS waiting lists are often six to eighteen months, while private provision is patchy and may be unaffordable. In this book the CBT skills required by trauma victims are elaborated: although learning skills from a book is not ideal, you may learn sufficient to make a difference. Further this book can help engage friends and relatives in your difficulties in a constructive way so that over time they can gently encourage you in moving on. To a degree the close friend or relative becomes the quasi-therapist in the community; while they may lack some of the technical knowledge of the therapist they do have the advantage of being available for much more than the hour-long sessions with the therapist spread over a couple of months.

What is EMDR?

The originator of eye movement desensitisation and reprocessing (EMDR), Francine Shapiro, a psychologist, was out walking one day in May 1987, when some disturbing thoughts came to her mind; they then seemed to fade away, coming back a little later but in a less disturbing way (Shapiro 1995). She puzzled as to how this had happened and realised that the emotional charge of the thoughts faded when she made diagonal eye movements. Over the next six months she experimented with friends and colleagues to see if the strategy worked for them. Her focus at that time was on the minor stresses of her associates, frustrations at work or memories of childhood humiliations. Encouraged by the results she went on to refine the strategy for people who had experienced extreme trauma.

What is the format of EMDR treatment sessions?

The early sessions of EMDR are little different from those in CBT in that the client verbalises the story of the trauma and before. However, in preparation for the eye movements they are also introduced to the notion of a 'safe place'. The safe place is somewhere that the client can retreat to if they are finding recounting the trauma too painful. The therapist carefully tailors the 'safe place' so that it is meaningful to the particular client. For example for one person it might be 'being in the kitchen with grandmother on a Sunday morning with the smell of eggs and bacon': when feeling overwhelmed they can 'visit'. Eye movements are usually not introduced until about the fourth session. The target initially is either a minor aspect of the trauma or minor stressor, such that using a distress scale 0–10, where 10 is maximum stress, the stress would be rated about a 7, i.e. a moderate rather than a severe stressor. Focusing on the moderate stressor, eye movements may be induced in a variety of ways, e.g. the client tracks the therapist's finger across their field of vision about twelve inches away from their face, or tracks a light beam as it moves along a tube. Typically between fifteen and twenty movements are made, then the client has a break while being briefly invited to describe anything that came to mind. The set of eye movements is repeated and followed with a break to describe the content of anything that had come up. These procedures are repeated until the distress score is reduced to 0 or 1. If the procedure is successful over moderate stressors, progress is made to the more extreme stressors. The client can indicate by a prearranged signal if they are finding the procedure too painful; it is then stopped and they can mentally visit the 'safe place'. Treatment sessions are typically sixty to ninety minutes and usually between one and four sessions are devoted to eye movements.

Curiously it has been found that eye movements are not essential to the efficacy of EMDR: any form of bilateral stimulation works equally well, e.g. the therapist tapping alternately on the client's hand, or listening to music in which the sound is played alternately into each ear. The biological mechanism by which EMDR facilitates the processing of traumatic material is unclear. From a psychological point of view it seems likely that the active ingredients in EMDR are that it involves some degree of exposure therapy and also the opportunity to reflect on the trauma as if it really was something from the past, 'an old movie', and not something that is happening now. Thus EMDR appears a variant of CBT.

When EMDR therapists work with clients with repeated childhood trauma, the cognitive elements become more explicit and the therapists borrow heavily from the armoury of CBT therapists when treating clients with personality disorders. As EMDR has evolved, it has absorbed developments in CBT so that it is much less clear what the unique contribution of the former is. It seems likely, however, that EMDR is a good way of titrating the dose of exposure to traumatic material so that a person can absorb it into their life story.

5

Resetting the alarm

At present you probably feel that you are operating in a war zone, with a sense that something terrible is going to happen, but you don't know quite what. Logically you might explain to yourself that realistically nothing bad is going to happen today, but the sense of vulnerability and threat persists. In Chapter 2 it was explained that this is because of your dodgy or hypersensitive alarm (amygdala). In this chapter the resetting of the alarm is addressed.

The land of avoidance

Most of those suffering after a trauma inhabit a land of avoidance, particularly anything associated with their trauma. Cecilia for example was avoiding driving on motorways after her accident. But the avoidance is not necessarily just associated with the trauma: it spreads into other areas and Cecilia was avoiding contact with her friends and sisters. She had also avoided playing badminton; initially this was because of her whiplash injuries but now she simply could not be bothered.

The other characters we met in Chapter 1 also emigrated to this land after their trauma. Like Cecilia they protest that it is the only safe place, but then wonder why it feels so like a prison cell. As Kevin put it, it is 'dead safe, scarcely moving out of my living room since the assault'. The prospects of leaving this land fill the inhabitants with images of catastrophes. Occasionally, rather like making a New Year resolution, a resident will tire of the supposed sanctuary, climb the dividing wall into the land of approach, go deep inside to those parts that they knew well before the trauma, only to discover that they find this such a frightening experience that they vow never again to climb the wall.

Not long after Cecilia's accident, she was invited to her niece's wedding, a two-hour drive away, and she felt she had to go. She travelled there as a passenger with her husband driving, felt just moderately stressed for the first forty minutes, and then blind panic set in for the remainder of the journey. Her husband Dave was irritated by her instructions and furious that she wanted to complete the return journey using A and B roads, forsaking the motorway. She felt more estranged from him for his 'lack of understanding'. Back at home she resolved never again to travel on a motorway and to stay 'secure' in the land of avoidance.

It is as if the permanent residents of the land of approach are a strange breed and are out of place in the land of avoidance. Unfortunately avoidance has a way of catching up on you.

Angela studiously avoided any conversations about abuse as well as TV programmes but she then encountered an advertisement from the National Society for the Prevention of Cruelty to Children (NSPCC) featuring a father looking into a bedroom, seeing his wife asleep, then walking to his daughter's room. The advert triggered reminders of her abuse by her father and left her distressed for the remainder of the evening. Although she married and had two children, she married largely to escape from home, sexual contact with her husband brought back memories of her abuse, so she avoided it and the marriage broke down. Angela was too afraid to embark on any subsequent intimate relationship.

The land of approach

This is the country that you probably inhabited before your trauma but it seems bizarre now. It is rather like being a convert to a new religious or political perspective: what felt so obviously right now seems utterly incongruous. Now it is as if you know about this land only at an intellectual level and what is now central to your identity is your trauma this defines you and consequently you may feel, like Cecilia, 'flawed, defective, worthless'.

Cecilia learnt that one of her sisters had to go into hospital for a few days. Cecilia was ashamed that she was more concerned about having to make conversation with the staff and visitors, if she visited, than with thoughts of her sister's plight. In addition the hospital was the same one that she had been taken to after her accident and Cecilia wanted to avoid this reminder. Cecilia reflected that before her trauma she would have been the first to visit someone in hospital.

Moving to 'approach'

People soon become disenchanted with living in the land of avoidance. They may well muse 'What sort of a life is it?', but instead of trekking to the border and making brief short forays into the land of approach, they parachute into the interior, frighten themselves and resolve never again to leave the land of avoidance.

A few months after her accident Cecilia pushed herself to visit her youngest sister, who had just had her first child; this necessitated driving thirty miles by motorway. By the time she arrived at her sister's house, she was totally drained. Cecilia was so preoccupied with the return journey that she did not enjoy the visit and resolved on the second leg never to use motorways.

Cecilia noted that she was in critical mode in teaching herself to relearn to drive but operated entirely differently in teaching her younger daughter Abigail to swim. The first few times she took Abigail to the pool she would simply splash water on her as she stood on the side, then progressed to Abigail jumping in, etc. Her driving thirty miles on the motorway was the equivalent of throwing her daughter in the deep end, an experience likely to be so frightening that she would never attend the pool again.

In terms of her 'dodgy alarm' (see Chapter 2) in driving to

her sister's house, Cecilia had tried to yank the alarm from the 'war zone' position to her safe place without going though intermediate places, e.g. the 'the risky neighbourhood' position. To reset the alarm, it is necessary to trip it, but in such a way that the distress is not overwhelming and commitment to tripping the alarm is maintained.

Committing to 'dares'

A commitment to anything, keeping fit or studying for an exam, will involve inevitable setbacks and this has to be budgeted for in advance to avoid demoralisation. Progress with dares can be likened to climbing a ladder, the next step is taken only when you are secure on the previous rung. Sometimes the gap between two rungs turns out to be larger than you anticipated or can manage, but importantly this does not mean that you are at the bottom of the ladder merely that you have to introduce an in-between step, get comfortable with that extra rung before trying the next rung. How much progress you make will depend on how much training you do.

Cecilia decided that she would do some training each time she drove, involving at least a dare a trip, and that she would keep a record of how bad the dare was on a scale 0 to 10, where 10 was awful. Her ultimate goal was to be able to drive on the motorway at peak time to her sisters with her children in the car. Cecilia's rough training programme is shown in Figure 5.1.

For Cecilia the first rung of the ladder consisted of not slowing down when the traffic lights were on amber en route to her local shop and not slowing down when she saw a car coming out of a side road. The first time she did each of these her score was 8/10 but by her sixth attempt her scores were down to 6/10, which she felt was manageable. She was then ready to attempt the next rung of the ladder, not to hesitate at the island that she encountered daily just before she got to work. To her surprise Cecilia found that this wasn't as stressful as she thought it was going to be and she rated it 6/10. Originally Cecilia had planned that the next rung of the ladder was to

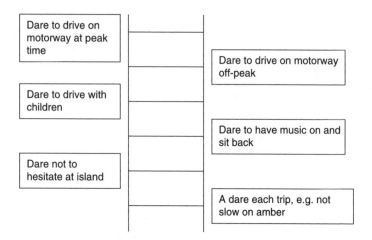

Figure 5.1 Cecilia's training schedule.

have music on in the car, but after discussion with her husband Dave, she realised that since the accident she had introduced other 'safety' procedures such as scanning from side to side and to counter this she agreed also to dare herself to focus on the colour of a car about five cars ahead. While she found it relatively easy to sing to music, she found it very difficult to keep focused on the horizon (five cars ahead) and it wasn't until about her tenth attempt that her score came to 6/10. Unfortunately, just as she had managed to stop scanning, she had to brake sharply and was so distressed that she became unnerved again at roundabouts. In effect she dropped down a rung of the ladder. Cecilia had to again dare herself to tackle the roundabout without hesitation, and she was disappointed that her stress level for this was now 8/10 and it wasn't until she had done this a dozen times that her score reached 6/10.

She then again attempted the next rung of the ladder, sitting back when driving, which she accomplished with ease. Cecilia also found that she wasn't as fearful as she anticipated when driving her children on A roads. However, she found that she had panic symptoms at the thought of driving on the motorway off peak. She therefore decided to introduce an intermediate step (not shown in Figure 5.1), driving on a motorway by herself on a Sunday morning, and spent a few weeks getting herself comfortable with this before attempting the next rung. Cecilia became increasingly aware that not only did she have to learn to tolerate some discomfort in resetting her alarm but also she had to pace herself for a marathon and not a sprint with inevitable setbacks. However, she was in control of the pace of training and she was only daring herself to drive in the style she did before, which unlike her present style enabled her to get from one place to another without exhaustion, and without really knowing how she had got there.

Cecilia also decided to tackle her fear as a passenger and she practised by keeping a focus on a car five cars ahead (thus reducing scanning), using a personal radio and singing along, and negotiating a fixed penalty with her husband if she issued instructions.

In post-traumatic stress disorder the person's fears are not confined to something obviously connected to the trauma. For example Cecilia not only had her fear of driving and difficulty as a passenger but also she was fearful of something happening to her younger daughter, Abigail. While Abigail was asleep at night, she would look in to see if she was OK at least twice. She therefore dared herself initially to look in only once. Although this left her agitated and her sleep worsened, she realised that she needed to tolerate this discomfort for long-term gain. It took her two weeks before her sleep returned to normal and she was then able to attempt not looking in on Abigail at all. Cecilia's sense of being in a 'war zone' also meant that when she left her home she would return several times to check that she really had locked her door, and if out with her husband, she would ring her older daughter Amanda to check that she and Abigail were OK. She weaned herself off checking the door by mentally putting a strange label on it such as 'green igloo' so that when she was tempted to check again, the incongruous phrase reminded her that she had completed the task. Cecilia found it very difficult to wean herself off ringing home but on one occasion, Amanda was very abrupt with her because she had rung only thirty minutes earlier. However, she realised that there could never be enough reassurance and even if she rang every fifteen minutes she would still be anxious. Cecilia was addicted to reassurance and she resolved to dare herself not to ring home when she was out.

Kevin's avoidance was also pervasive: since he was assaulted he had become a virtual recluse, venturing only to his local shop unaccompanied. At home he was very fearful, keeping his curtains closed at all times and peeping through them to check on any visitors before opening his door to them. He would repeatedly check that his cooker was switched off and each time he would stare at it to ensure that the dial was indeed pointing to the off position. Since the assault he also insisted on unplugging all appliances before going to bed. Kevin had been unable to return to his work in the Tax Office since the assault and was now on half pay, which in turn was creating financial difficulties. He realised he could not go on being a hermit. He constructed the rough training programme shown in Figure 5.2.

Kevin was not amused when he opened his front door to his brother to be greeted with 'Still playing "peek a boo" are we?' Later Kevin realised he had to make a start on not looking through his curtains to identify his visitor before opening his front door and thought it would look less absurd if he had his curtains open. After about thirty minutes of leaving his curtains open, he felt very vulnerable and went to unwind by taking a shower. When he returned to his living room, he pondered that

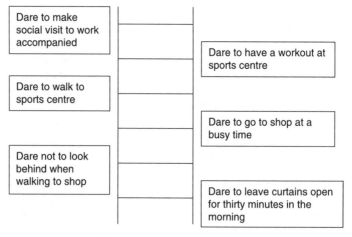

Figure 5.2 Kevin's training schedule.

at least he had left his curtains open for thirty minutes and resolved to do this every day until he felt at ease with it.

He had noticed that he attracted stares by looking behind him a couple of times when he walked to his local shop. Kevin decided that en route to the shop he would keep focused on a spot 20 yards ahead, a behaviour incompatible with looking behind. He found that within ten days he could walk to the shop without looking around.

His next challenge was to go to the shop at a busy time: this worked fine the first time and he rated his anxiety at 7/10. However, on his next attempt the shopkeeper and a customer were arguing and despite it not involving him he was very agitated, rated at 9/10 when he got home. He was tempted to revert to going to the shop at quiet times but then resolved that he was not going to be 'bullied' into avoiding busy times, though he was not quite sure who the bully was. Week by week Kevin progressed up his ladder until finally he had gone to the gym with his brother and began his workout. His brother expressed astonishment that Kevin began his routine where he had finished before his assault and told him in no uncertain terms that he was going to injure himself with such heavy weights at this stage. Kevin was initially annoyed with his brother but then realised that, in view of his long absence, over the weeks he should gradually progress from free standing exercises, to exercise machines and then to weights. As he reverted to free standing exercises, he pondered that in a similar fashion for 'safety' he should have a more graded approach to his return to work. He decided that the next rung on his ladder should not be returning to work but paying a social visit to work (top rung of Figure 5.2) and after that there should be a yet further stepping stone of returning to work on light duties.

The key point about 'dares' is that they enable you to legitimise your way of operating before the trauma, not just at an intellectual level of, for example, 'I suppose it must have been OK to drive the way I did before the accident or to go to the gym' but also at an experiential level of 'I feel safe with my normal driving or going to the gym'. Any departure from your pre-trauma way of operating is taken by the amygdala as evidence that you must be in a 'war zone' with a resulting sense of vulnerability or threat. It is therefore crucially important to wean you off so-called 'safety' behaviours that you have developed since the trauma.

Angela tackled her avoidance by first refusing to be bullied into switching TV channels when items related to abuse featured. She then decided to join a creative writing group where she might encounter males. After she was comfortable in the group she decided to reciprocate mild flirtations with male members. Finally, she agreed to go on a date, reminding herself of the similarities and differences between her date and her father. When she got anxious with her date, she played 'spot the difference'.

Saboteurs

As you begin to journey into the land of approach you will probably encounter saboteurs, which come in a variety of shapes and sizes. First, for some trauma victims, there is an inner critical voice seeking to sabotage their efforts. Sometimes this voice is very insistent, particularly so when they attempt to move up a rung of the ladder. If you 'hear' this 'voice' it does not mean that you have a severe mental illness but it can hinder your progress if it is not taken with a 'pinch of salt'. The second saboteur can involve extreme negative descriptions of yourself (e.g. 'flawed') and your surroundings (e.g. 'dangerous') since the trauma. The third saboteur may involve toxic accompaniments of your dares – flashbacks and/or dreams of your trauma and panic attacks. Basic strategies for neutralising the saboteurs are discussed below.

The critical voice
Often the negative self-critical internal dialogue can be crystallised into a 'voice' as if it was another 'you' whose motivation can be challenged as well as the accuracy of what is spoken.

Kevin varied in how he thought of this voice: sometimes he thought of his having a 'devil' on one shoulder always urging inaction and repeated checking and an 'angel' on the other shoulder urging the opposite. At other times he thought of two competing voices, 'Kevin mark 1' who had his interests at heart and was encouraging him to gradually approach life speaking in soft tones, and 'Kevin mark 2' speaking harshly and critically, telling him to avoid things and at times having tantrums. During his first return workout at the gym, 'Kevin mark 2' came on stream with 'What is the point in this, you thought you were a big strong lad but you couldn't defend yourself in the assault, look at you now doing free standing exercises' and he switched his attention to 'Kevin mark 1', who was saying 'You have made a start, it is a marathon, but if you keep up this nice steady pace you will get there'. He decided to stay with 'Kevin mark 1' because he knew he was trustworthy.

Sam's demon voice was different from Kevin's in that it was alternately seductive, 'Just have a drink, it will calm you, one will do no harm' and incredulous, 'What do you think you are doing driving, it's not that you are a bad driver, it's how others drive, you've no control at all'. In many ways Sam's demon voice was more difficult for him to deal with because it had a veneer of rationality and calm. Once he had properly identified it, he called it the carbon monoxide voice – deadly but with no smell. Whereas he saw listening to 'Sam's voice' as opening a window on a summer's day to the fragrance of roses. He practised switching his attention from the 'insidious gas' to the 'rose' to enable him to tackle his driving, using a ladder similar to that of Cecilia in Figure 5.1. Further he understood that he could not reset his alarm if it was 'pickled in alcohol'.

Patrick's inner saboteur was different again: he viewed it as the 'Old Codger' constantly ruminating, 'I remember when I used to . . .' to the total boredom of all those around him, including himself. He decided that the appropriate response was for the real Patrick to yawn and stretch and excuse himself, 'I've just got to make the best of the next thirty minutes by, say, potting some plants in the greenhouse'.

Maureen was determined to overcome her phobia about travelling on a bus, but as soon as she approached a bus stop by herself a little voice seemed to say, 'You are going to fall getting on', even though she had never done so, albeit that she wasn't as steady on her feet as she had been some years ago. When the voice spoke, she could feel herself falling and her stomach would turn. She decided to see this voice as that of her very severe Aunt Janet who she knew in childhood and test out whether this 'battleaxe' was right or wrong by daring herself to board a bus alone. Since being thrown forward on the bus, Maureen also found that in a supermarket, when pushing a trolley, she would stop to let others go past and realised this only when a friend pointed it out and she became annoyed with herself. To cope with this, Maureen took it that it was actually 'Aunt Jane' being hypercritical while she was stopping and that it did not really matter for now if she was hesitant. It simply meant that for the time being her 'dodgy alarm' was not quite back to the 'safe place' position.

An exaggeratedly negative view of yourself and your personal world

After a major trauma you may take a picture of yourself and your world from a rather odd angle. The picture will bear some relationship to reality but it is rather like a bad passport photograph and it may stop you venturing out to do dares. The intent is not to produce a photograph that flatters but one that is more realistic. Our emotions are very much influenced by how we set our camera the lenses and filters we choose.

Prior to being shot, Ian was very aware that his world could be a dangerous place but afterwards he saw himself as on a 'battlefield'. Although he knew he was not the target, he feared the gunmen might think he recognised them and seek him out; consequently he saw himself as 'vulnerable'. He behaved initially as if home was the only 'safe place', and then realised that he was so well known from his amateur boxing days that it would be easy to find his address. Further given that nothing had happened to him in the eighteen months of being a 'sitting duck', he began to doubt whether a 'battlefield' description was appropriate. This freed him to attempt some dares. However, Ian continued to see the club he worked at and any other club as the 'battlefront'.

Karen had had a low opinion of herself since ever she could

remember, but after the rapes it turned to hate and a mistrust of all males. Although she had always had a good relationship with her parents, she would not let them babysit her daughter any longer. Her mood was deteriorating as she ran out of excuses. She felt she could no longer trust her judgement not only about males but also about what were appropriate clothes to buy. Karen decided that she would make the first rung of her ladder (see Figure 5.1) buying a style of jacket that she had bought before the rape and the next rung was to ask her parents to mind her daughter for an hour after school.

Pedro saw himself as 'stupid' for stubbing cigarettes out on himself: he had begun to do this as a 12 year old following years of physical abuse by his father. Originally he wanted to feel something rather than experience his numbness or empti- ness. He told himself it was inappropriate behaviour now because he could feel some warmth to his wife and son but this increased his feelings of 'stupidity' when he slipped and stubbed a cigarette out on himself. Pedro also berated himself for his heart racing and sweating a little when he heard the voices of males raised. He realised that there was a big gap between how he looked at himself and how his wife and son viewed him. Pedro decided that it would probably be more helpful to view himself through the eyes of his wife and son rather than through his father's eyes. With his wife's encouragement he dared himself to make a start on compen- sating for his missed education by attending English and Maths classes, even though the teacher for the latter was a male.

In the year before her climbing accident, Sandra had been the top performer in the law firm that she worked for and received a financial bonus for this, but for the two years since then, her work had been deemed simply acceptable. She had felt very low over this and her confidence in general had ebbed away so much that she pulled out of the sale of her flat, despite clear evidence that the buying of a new property was financially viable. When talking to a senior colleague, she realised that the performance of most staff in any one year was rated as 'acceptable' and this challenged her belief that 'If I am not the top then I am a flop'. She then dared herself to once again put her flat on the market.

Toxic accompaniments of dares

Daring yourself to attempt what you have been avoiding can trigger flashbacks and nightmares of your trauma or sometimes panic attacks. The skill is to approach what you did previously in such a gradual way that these intrusions are not overwhelming and panic symptoms are treated with a detached mindfulness. Panic attacks can be viewed as the tripping of a hypersensitive amygdala (alarm) in response to any unusual (but not abnormal) internal sensation, e.g. heart racing, while flashbacks often occur in response to external triggers that in some way seem to match the trauma that created the 'dodgy alarm'.

Joan had become scared to go out alone since she was mugged. At the mere thought of going out by herself, she would experience palpitations, start sweating, feel faint and need to sit down. During these attacks she felt that she was going to lose control and on a couple of occasions had been taken to her local Accident and Emergency Department by her family because she thought she was having a heart attack. She then realised that if she could bring on these symptoms just by thinking about going out, they could not be that serious as no one could talk themselves into a heart attack or stroke. Joan decided to see her panic symptoms as a 'Big Dipper' experience. Going up one side of the ride, she could feel herself experiencing more symptoms and each one more intensely, but if she saw them simply as a nuisance and not a catastrophe, the symptoms would subside as the ride passed the peak. She concluded that the ride lasted no more than about ten minutes, roughly the length of time she might spend in the dentist's chair, and that her discomfort in the attacks was no more significant than that of being in the dentist's. Although the attacks lasted only ten minutes, she would spend most of the day thinking about how awful they were and when the next one would be; she now saw that this was pointless agonising, rather like constantly picking at a sore, with the inflammation from the picking becoming worse than the sore itself.

She resolved to stop 'picking', switching her attention calmly elsewhere to her music.

For Joan the first rung of the ladder for her dares was to dare herself not to sit down during an attack. In this way she collected experimental evidence that her fear that she would faint was unfounded. Once she became comfortable managing these attacks at home, she progressed to the next rung, daring herself to walk by herself to her friend and neighbour a few doors away. Subsequently she went to her local shops with her neighbour and Joan dared herself to go into one shop by herself while her friend went into an adjacent shop. They planned to meet in a nearby coffee shop afterwards. However, in the shop Joan began to experience the panic symptoms but insisted that she would tolerate them by viewing her body as on a 'Big Dipper' ride and she would not, as it were, climb off the ride at the top by running out of the shop.

John returned to work six months after a gas explosion there. He had some minor burns from the incident, which had largely healed by three months, and he began driving past the plant. He felt nauseous as he did so, but less so with repetition. On his return to work John was alarmed that as he passed the Occupational Health Department, just inside the plant gates and where he was taken initially after the explosion, he had a flashback of the ball of flame coming towards him, as if in slow motion, and thinking that he was going to die. He was very agitated when he arrived to meet with colleagues in the rest room and could 'feel' the burns from the time of the explosion. John knew this was 'crazy', as his burns had healed. John was distracted from the intrusive flashback by banter with a colleague, which lifted his mood sufficiently to think of a game plan to keep such intrusions at a manageable distance. While he was tempted to go home, he realised that this was not a real solution as he sometimes had such flashbacks there when he saw an explosion on TV. He decided that when he experienced the ball of flame coming towards him and remembered rolling on the ground to put the flames out, he would imagine being given an anaesthetic and feel the anaesthetic first flowing into the areas that were burnt and then his body becoming numb and rubbery, rather like parts of his face could stay 'rubbery' after a visit to the dentist. Importantly John's strategy was not to try and blank or run away from the flashback, as he had found this brought only temporary relief, followed by a more intense flashback. The traumatic memory was on an elastic band and the harder he pushed it away, the more strongly it rebounded. The 'anaesthetic' routine enabled John to at least stay in work and he decided that the next rung of the ladder would be to enter the workshop where the explosion had occurred, but at lunch times when no gas cylinders were being used for welding. Then he would progress to the next rung of the ladder, entering the workshop at coffee breaks when there was little activity with cylinders.

Peter, like John, was afraid to return to work following his trauma. In part it served as a reminder of his colleague's head being crushed in the fall from the scaffolding, but he was also afraid to get close to any colleague lest a similar fate befell them. He felt he couldn't stand to go through the same emotions again. Peter realised that his emotional avoidance was constricting his life, creating financial problems and also stopping him celebrating with others to the extent that he had stopped watching football matches on TV with his son because he could not tolerate the uncertainty. He decided that the first rung on his ladder was to watch football on TV with his son and the second rung would be to return to work but visiting different sites so that he did not get 'too attached'. When he returned to work, he was fine at the times of the day when there was little activity above him on the scaffolding but at busy times he had flashbacks of the incident, the smell of the dust around, the stickiness of the blood and a deep sense of guilt. It occurred to him that his son, who wanted to be a surveyor, could encounter exactly the same situation as he had encountered and were he to do so, he would comfort him by saying, 'You did all you could, no one could ask more, hang in there'. Peter decided to repeat this to himself each time he had a flashback. The next rung of the ladder was to dare himself to stay under scaffolding at a time when it was busy. The final rung of the ladder for Peter was to take a job role that was based entirely at one site.

Bob, like John and Peter, had memories of his trauma triggered by the workplace. After his experience of being bullied at work, he felt he could never again be an employee but had resolved to make a business of his hobby of making doll's houses. He went to see his bank manager in the hope of securing some pump-priming finance, but found that he wasn't taking in what the manager said because Bob was preoccupied with the manager's brusqueness, which made him think of his boss cursing him. Bob came out of the meeting in a bewildered state. Fortunately his wife had been present and to his surprise, she thought it had been a positive meeting in that the manager had simply requested a business plan before making a decision. Further she reminded him that, unlike his boss, the bank manager had not raised his voice, had not cursed and was a lot older. Bob resolved that when he had flashbacks to the bullying, he would go through a list of things that made the current situation different from before – similar to the childhood game of 'spot the difference'. For Bob the next rung of the ladder was to put this trauma discrimination into practice at the next meeting with his bank manager. A loan was negotiated and Bob realised that he would likely get flashbacks negotiating with estate agents regarding premises and having to deal with solicitors. In order to deal with this rung of the ladder, he would have to remind himself of the similarities and differences of these people compared to his boss.

Although relieved that her unborn baby had not been harmed by her tripping as she got out of a taxi, Emma had become very fearful walking along pavements. She would walk with her head down scrutinising the road surface and was preoccupied with thoughts that something could have happened to the baby and she would not have been able to forgive herself. Since the original fall she had fallen twice, necessitating a visit to the Accident and Emergency Department on the first occasion and one to her GP on the second occasion. The latter explained to her that human beings look to the horizon to keep their balance and it was therefore not surprising if she tripped looking at her feet, particularly if she was engaged in watching a horror video of what did not happen. Emma decided to dare herself to walk along the pavement with her eyes on the horizon for just a minute and found that this was easier than she expected. She thought that the next rung of the ladder would be to do the same for the five minute walk from her home to her mother's home. However, as this walk progressed she first began to ponder the horror video and then felt guilty that she had been restricting her son's life by not journeying by taxi. She resolved to calmly switch 'channels' to a reality video when she found herself unthinkingly watching the horror video. Emma decided that the rungs of the ladder to be climbed in ascending order would first be to travel by taxi with her husband, then to travel alone and the final step would be to take a taxi with the baby.

Both Amanda and Abigail were obliged to get lifts from their parents to their respective schools, but were more fearful if only their mother, Cecilia, was available to take them, as this triggered memories of the accident. Further, the children would make comments about safety to their mother, who would in turn become irate. Matters were compounded because it was their mother who took them to Morris Dancing competitions at weekends in the season. With their father's encouragement both girls were 'dared' to travel with their mother but to replace or at least minimise the fear by singing with gusto to their favourite music on their portable media players. Initially they adopted this strategy en route to school and the next rung was to use it with longer journeys at weekends.

6

Better ways of handling the traumatic memory

For many people their traumatic memory feels as if it happened yesterday. It is so vivid, they remember not only what happened, but also the sights, sounds and smells associated with the event. When it comes to mind they may re-experience many of the bodily sensations that they had at the time of the incident, for example the sense of helplessness or horror. These flashbacks may occur in response to some reminder or may come out of the blue. At their worst, but rarely, the flashbacks may be so extreme that the person loses awareness of their surroundings for a time: these are *dissociative flashbacks*. Further your sleep may be disturbed by dreams of the incident and sometimes the dreams are of an even worse outcome. You may wake in a distressed state, have difficulty getting back to sleep and fearful of a reoccurrence of the nightmare if you do return to sleep. The nightmares may even affect your mood the next day.

How do you handle your traumatic memories?

If flashbacks are a problem for you, the likelihood is that you use one of the coping strategies in Table 6.1. These strategies do work but only very briefly. Minutes later the memory is back and often stronger and more vivid. You might try your favourite strategy from Table 6.1 again, get temporary relief but then are haunted by an even more vivid image. If alcohol is your favoured coping strategy, it is easy to see how it can become a problem but equally though less obviously, the habitual use of the other strategies in Table 6.1 may result in

Table 6.1 **Ineffective coping strategies**

- Trying to think of something else
- Trying to think of something nice
- Getting up and going into another room
- Going to do something
- Talking to someone about anything other than the incident
- Having a drink of alcohol
- Taking other drugs

your total frustration and a sense that you are losing the plot. This is doubly frustrating if you have always prided yourself on being a strong, sensible and organised person.

Using one or more of the strategies in Table 6.1 may have become second nature to you and letting go of them can be difficult: old habits die hard. The first step is recognising that the above strategies do not actually work. This recognition can be obscured because the coping strategies in Table 6.1 make a great deal of common sense. But then when you ask yourself, 'How long have I been using one or more of the strategies in Table 6.1? Where has using the strategies got me?' they seem less credible. What is needed is a commitment to letting go of these strategies tempered by a realisation that it will almost certainly be a question of two steps forward and one back as you learn better ways of handling the disturbing memories.

Viewing traumatic memories as a bully

Traumatic memories can operate as a bully upsetting you when you 'see' them, fearful of what they might do. A great deal of energy is spent trying to avoid the bullying, leaving little energy to get on and enjoy ordinary life. Running away from the bully seems to be the obvious strategy but just makes matters worse in the end. Yet the mere thought of confronting the bully makes you feel ill. Fortunately there are a variety of ways of facing the demon so that it loses its power, and we'll look at them in the rest of this chapter.

Having the last word

Managing the bully requires subtlety rather than head-on confrontation: better ways of handling the traumatic memory are summarised in Table 6.2. Looking at Table 6.2 the strategies can seem simple enough but they do require a great deal of practice, with usually some frustration and pain to begin with. You may find some strategies or combination of strategies more suited to you than others.

The goal of the effective coping strategies is not to eliminate the traumatic memory. Unfortunately the brain is not like the hard drive of your computer where you can simply delete a file: the memory is still there, but by using appropriate strategies, your response may ensure discomfort rather than great upset. It is best to work down the list of strategies in Table 6.2 starting from the top. How far down you would need to go before you reach a point of being able to 'see' the bully without distress is impossible to judge in advance; it is a question of gentle experimentation. To guide you in this experimentation, examples of how the characters in this book surmounted the stumbling blocks are detailed. Despite this you may reach a point where you seem to be 'stuck' as you begin your descent of Table 6.2, and you may need professional help to unhook you. Even if this happens, you know the terrain well and the therapist can home in on your specific difficulties and will not need to spend much, if any, time educating you about the nature of trauma and its effects.

Table 6.2 **Effective coping strategies**

- Acknowledging the memory at a distance
- Stopping rumination
- Daring to mention the trauma
- Dictating the story of the trauma and its effects
- Rereading the story at a special time
- Writing about it and its consequences at a special time

Acknowledging the memory at a distance

In the weeks and months after an extreme trauma, the memory can feel overwhelming: this is a normal reaction to an abnormal event. For most people, over time, the traumatic memory gradually becomes more manageable. It seems likely that there is a natural healing process, what Wells and Sembi (2004) have termed *reflexive adaptive processing*. If a person continues to use the ineffective coping strategies listed in Table 6.1, it interferes with reflexive adaptive processing, leading to chronic symptoms. To reinstate reflexive adaptive processing, it is necessary to wean yourself off the ineffective strategies in Table 6.1 and cultivate a detached mindfulness about the intrusions, rather as on a summer's day one might be watching clouds drift by: although aware of them, you are actually thinking of something else. In this way the memory of the trauma can be processed at a safe distance. [A similar phenomenon probably accounts for the effectiveness of EMDR, in which there is a dual focus on eye movements (or some other bilateral stimulation such as finger tapping on alternate hands) and the traumatic memory.] It is as if the traumatic memory is a fire: putting it out isn't an option, it is raging, but it can be contained at a safe distance.

Pedro, an avid football supporter, was struck by how useful it was to have slow motion action replays of goals scored so that the side that had conceded the goal could learn from the mistake. He decided to apply the same strategy to his stubbing cigarettes out on himself. Pedro noticed that this behaviour was often preceded by an image of seeing his mother attacked by his father when he was aged 11. For Pedro, this was the last straw: he threw himself at his father, knocking him backwards, his head hit a shelf and began bleeding profusely, his father went berserk but Pedro had time to swing his cricket bat at his father's legs, immobilising him while he and his mother escaped and went to stay with his maternal grandmother. This was to be the last occasion that he saw his father. When they returned a week later, he had left and Pedro remembered trying to clean the blood off his desk (which was under the shelf) and feeling guilty that he had driven his father away.

Flashbacks of this evoked both sadness that he had 'lost' his father and anger at him. Pedro thought that it was this mix of emotions that led to his stubbing cigarettes out on himself. He realised that he was still letting his father 'bully' him by responding to the memory of the last day in this self-destructive way. Pedro decided on a strategy of detached mindfulness about the last day. He would acknowledge it as he would have greeted a known bully at school: blanking them wasn't an option but by the same token he did not want to be involved with them. He was not going to let his father have the last word in what he did. When memories of his abuse came to mind, he would view it as an old black and white movie that he would simply let play in the background while he got on with his day-to-day activities. He realised that he only made matters worse on the occasions he tried to operate an 'off' button for the movie.

Bob had flashbacks of his boss at work bullying him, and realised that in a sense his boss was still present bullying him. Bob was able to distance himself from this image by the realisation that it had no power: it could not dictate when he had a coffee break or when he went to bed, it was simply an image of something that had happened in the past. Bob imagined his life as a timeline with various pictures located along it, winning a swimming gala at age 13, getting married at 22, and the image of his boss was located at a point three years ago. When troubled by the memory of his boss being abusive to him, he would simply locate it along the timeline and focus simultaneously on making the most of the next thirty minutes, allowing his boss to fade of his own accord.

Sam had difficulty distancing himself from the memory of his car accident because he tended to drink alcohol, which in turn made him morose and he would then dwell on it. He tried to stop drinking all at once, but had such severe withdrawal symptoms such as shaking and nausea that he recommenced drinking. Sam then consulted his GP, who suggested that he take tranquilisers just for the two to three weeks needed to withdraw from alcohol and that he would then similarly taper him off the tranquilisers to avoid dependence. Following this Sam was able to see the memory of his accident as if he were a passenger on a train and the trauma as the surrounding countryside, mindful of it, but not really absorbed by it.

Stopping rumination

Thoughts following an extreme trauma may focus not only on the specifics of 'What happened? When? With what emotion?' but lead on to over-general thinking such as 'I am a mess, always have been'. Over-general thinking is characteristic of people with PTSD and depression. The traumatic memory and the self concept interact, thus if the latter is negative it can colour the perception of what happened, particularly if the person agonises about their global indictment. Practising detached mindfulness requires a commitment not to agonise and to become skilled at switching the focus of attention (attention training) and to address the content of the ruminations at a set time if they still feel it is an issue at that time.

Pedro, Sam and Bob all dwelt on their inadequacies following flashbacks or dreams of their trauma. It was as if their trauma and the consequences were sores which they constantly picked at, and the inflammation that arose from picking was worse than the sore itself. Pedro and Bob particularly found that they tended to agonise when they were trying to get to sleep at night.

Bob decided to distract himself by setting his CD player such that it would flip from track to track, with just a minute of each track playing and let any traumatic memory float in and out again. He realised that this was not the time and place to agonise about his 'failure' to stand up to his boss and he postponed these considerations to a worry half-hour at 11 a.m. In fact by mid-morning, most of the time, what had been an issue the night before had evaporated. Bob reasoned that his boss wasn't worth more than thirty minutes a day.

As he was trying to get to sleep, Pedro stopped his ruminating by maintaining a dual focus on roving around the sounds available to him (the tick of the alarm clock, the rustling of leaves in the trees outside, the sound of traffic) and simply noting without comment any details of the traumatic memory that came to mind. He visualised his father as bait and himself as a fish swimming along smiling to himself when he saw the bait making a note to sort out his father on paper in a worry time the next day.

When Sam had flashbacks of his accident, he dwelt on his 'failure' to protect his children and would find himself 'picking' before he realised it; he found it amusing to recall his mother's voice snapping at him not to pick at his heat spots as a child. While he tried to let the memories of the accident float by, in the way he let the clouds in the sky pass by, he found this very difficult because they also evoked feelings of failure. It was not until he coupled this strategy with postponing these considerations to a fixed time that he was able keep the memory at an appropriate distance. By the time his 'failure' time came around, it sometimes felt a 'non-issue'. Sam was puzzled by this: it seemed that he was a failure some days but not others and that if he thought that one of his children had red hair one day and black another day, he would think there was something wrong in his judgement and that in a sense he was colour-blind about himself since the accident.

Daring to mention the trauma

Many trauma victims avoid talking about the incident/s or give all but the barest of details necessary for politeness. The more detail they go into, the more the memories come flooding back and they have a sense of being swept away on a tidal wave of emotion. But if post-traumatic stress symptoms are persisting, this emotional avoidance needs revisiting.

Other people may facilitate talking about it, if you, believe that they are genuinely interested in you, but you are likely to be dissuaded from doing so if you believe they are only concerned to know the morbid details. You are likely to be inhibited if the trauma involves a loss not only for yourself but also for those around you fearing upsetting them.

Approaching the second anniversary of her climbing accident, in which her partner Colin was killed, Sandra mused on how he seemed to have been forgotten. She got on well with his parents and still visited them, but felt that mentioning him was taboo. Her own mother had also been fond of Colin and she felt she couldn't mention him to her for fear of upsetting her. However, she decided that Colin deserved respect and she would invite her mother and his parents to visit his grave with her on the anniversary and go for lunch afterwards. It was upsetting for all at the graveside, but at lunch they were able to move on to share amusing anecdotes about Colin. Subsequently she was able to voice to his parents that she felt guilty for being alive and his mother comforted her, while his father underlined what Colin would be wanting her to do now. She resolved to become more active out of respect for Colin.

Dictating the story of the trauma and its effects

If you are suffering from post-traumatic stress disorder, you are not simply remembering your trauma but re-experiencing it, probably as if it happened yesterday, together with disturbing bodily sensations such as heart racing and breathlessness. In order for the trauma to become simply a bad memory, it has been found necessary to deliberately and repeatedly emotionally engage with the traumatic material (see Jaycox et al. 1998). This can seem strange as you may well think that you already battle with the memory, but your efforts are likely devoted to blocking the unbidden memory. It seems that deliberate and repeated engagement with the trauma memory helps the mind make a distinction between remembering and re-experiencing.

In *exposure treatment*, clients are asked to close their eyes and recount details of their trauma 'as if it were happening now', focusing on the details of the trauma as well as on their emotions and thoughts during the trauma. Exposure lasts for forty-five to sixty minutes each session; if clients finish recounting before the end of the time period, they are asked to go back to the beginning and start again. Each session, the client's narratives are audio-taped and clients are instructed to listen to the tapes once a day, imagining that the trauma is happening now, with attention to details of the trauma and their emotions and thoughts during it. The clients who do best are those who are very concrete and specific about their traumatic experience and who report distress at recounting their traumatic experience decreasing from session to session (a process termed *habituation*). Although exposure treatment has been found to be very effective, in routine clinical practice psychologists rarely provide it (Becker et al. 2004), despite awareness of it, largely because it is a distressing procedure. However, it is possible to borrow the essence of exposure treatment and use it as a self-help procedure, utilising a trusted friend or relative as opposed to a therapist.

In the immediate aftermath of an extreme trauma, most people feel that the memory is controlling them but if this persists, you are likely to feel increasingly helpless. Prior to the trauma there were likely other unpleasant life events, albeit that they were less dramatic, but you stamped your mark on them by working out what they meant about you and your personal world. For example, in order to get your bearings after say the break up of a relationship, you probably talked to friends and discussed how terrible your partner had been and whether your own idiosyncrasies played a part. In effect, you used others to complete a narrative, a story about yourself. This then gave direction to the next chapter in your autobiography, e.g. being more hesitant to commit in the next relationship.

Attempting to construct that chapter of your autobiography that deals with the extreme trauma has some added difficulties: first, there can be some aspects of what you experienced that are hard to find any words for or seem so bizarre that you worry others will think you are truly mad. Second, there can be some aspects that you will not verbalise to others because to do so would make it 'real', risking overwhelming you, while it just circulates in your own mind you can treat it more like an 'awake dream' rather an historical event. Third, you may feel that your extreme trauma is so unusual that no one around you who had not been through it could possibly understand it or its effects. Yet if this 'writer's block' is not surmounted, post-traumatic stress symptoms are likely to persist – PTSD involves arrested information processing.

It may be a struggle to express your experience, and the words may seem inadequate to begin with, but with practice you can better label your emotions. It is rather like giving a filename to a file on a computer: without such a label you are not able to access it properly or update its contents. You may feel that others will think you mad if you tell them of your experience, but test this out with one or two people who are close to you. The alternative is that the thoughts, images and feelings travel interminably around well-worn grooves in your mind, making for poor company: you try to avoid them but keep bumping into them. The task of the person you tell the story of the trauma and its effects to can never be to experience it as you did, but simply to visit the scene with you. You may recall perhaps visiting an aged and dying relative with a friend; afterwards you express your deep gratitude to them for their company, they might shuffle slightly embarrassed, protesting that they did not do anything or did not know what to say, but you dismiss this as being of no account, they were there. The presence of someone you trust and feel safe with helps ensure that you will not be overwhelmed by putting your trauma into words. Further it is as if you are in control of a valve that opens access to the traumatic memory: you control how much or how little you open the valve at any point in time. You can if you wish to begin with just open it a little so that it 'trickles' through; eventually you will let the complete story through. (If you are afraid of overwhelming your partner or friend with memories of the trauma, you can similarly 'trickle' the account.)

Narrating the story of the trauma can evoke feelings of helplessness that may resonate with those encountered at the time of the incident/s. It is therefore important to plan a change of gear that is a re-engagement in effective action, e.g. going for a brisk walk with your partner or friend at the end of dictation.

Many trauma victims start off with just a 'police' account of their extreme trauma, describing who was involved, when and where it happened, where you were taken afterwards. But if post-traumatic stress symptoms are persisting, it is important to move gradually beyond the official factual account to tell the story with emotion in a safe environment.

You may have always prided yourself on being able to sort out your own problems, but in the wake of the extreme trauma you may be struggling. If you continue to insist on the 'privacy' of your traumatic experience, despite the persistence of post-traumatic stress symptoms, you may be trapping yourself. While your own actions, such as the 'dares' described in Chapter 5, are crucial to reclaiming your life, a compulsive self-reliance can prevent you moving on. Viewing yourself as a failure if you share your experience may be an own goal. It may be particularly difficult to go public on your trauma if you have always restricted the expression of your feelings and experiences. You may need professional help to facilitate this: you would still be doing the work but the therapist would supply the tools. The strategies described in this book are a particular set of tools that you might use under your own steam. It is important not to blame yourself for not already having a 'toolbox'.

In Table 1.2 in Chapter 1, five headings were given to make a thumbnail stretch of your experiences (see page 21). You can turn this into the foundation of your story of the trauma and effects thus: 'I have flashbacks/nightmares of. . . . I avoid. . . . I keep thinking. . . . Being on edge has affected. . . . The worst part of what happened was. . . .' and dictating to a partner or friend what goes in the gaps. (You could of course just do it yourself, but you will probably find it less overwhelming to begin with to dictate it, and in so doing building bridges with those closest.)

When the dictation is repeated, you add in the 'superstructure', gradually filling in extra details or new angles on the trauma. Not only are you verbally dictating the trauma but also you are dictating the meaning of the trauma. Initially it will seem that the trauma speaks for itself the sights, sounds and feelings, but as you translate your experiences into communicable language, the meaning and action implications are distilled.

The first couple of times that you deliberately talk about the trauma and its effects can result in more flashbacks or dreams but usually after two or three weeks of daily practice you get a sense of completion, of having said all you can say, and there is a significant reduction in nightmares. One way of viewing dreams is that they represent material that has not been sorted out in the day. Thus by repeated dictation you are likely to reduce nightmares.

It was over a year since John had been involved in a gas explosion at work. His wife complained bitterly that since then he was in a world of his own, rarely initiating conversation and making monosyllabic responses to questions. She noticed however that there were times when he had a fixed stare and it was particularly difficult to get any response at such times. His stock response when asked what he was thinking was 'Nothing'. She decided to challenge this and asked for the ten-minute video that seemed to play while he had this stare. He was abrupt and replied, 'You do not want to know'. She responded with expletives that she did! It was agreed that he would make a start and she would write down what he said. John began to tell her about the gas explosion, but would reach a point where his stomach felt as if it had turned and dropped and he would have to stop his narrative. He could not explain why he experienced this sensation, and as far as he could remember this did not occur at the time of the explosion or at the same point in the story. Nevertheless they agreed to treat the stomach turning rather like a light flashing on the dashboard of a car: to override it might be dangerous, they needed to change direction and agreed to go for a walk together, switching attention to the trees, birds, children and ducks in the park. They viewed the walk in the park as a tuning into reality. In keeping with the framework of Table 1.2 in Chapter 1, John described the flashback of the ball of fire coming towards him in slow motion, but initially could not bring himself to describe his worst moment. On about the fifth day of dictating the trauma, his wife asked him, 'Was the worst moment when you thought you were going to die?' at which he broke down sobbing and she hugged him. He explained that in fact it wasn't so much he thought he was going to die as that at that time he was totally concerned about himself and didn't think at all about her or their children. She gently reminded him that one of the Psalms said that there was a time and a place for everything, a time for talking about the trauma, a time for using your energies to ensure survival and a time for focusing on her and the children.

Despite her troubled childhood, Angela had done well at school; it was a sanctuary from her toxic home. She had wanted to tell her teachers at secondary school what was going on, but was fearful of making matters worse at home. Later she studied for a degree part time and became interested in creative writing. She mused that though she had a wide range of life experience to draw upon, she chose to write more in the vein of the romantic novelist Danielle Steel, who similarly had a very troubled private life. Angela became aware that she was avoiding painful issues and decided to confront them in small doses, limiting herself to writing for no more than twenty minutes a day about her painful childhood and adolescent experiences. The writing made the experiences more vivid than usual and her sleep worsened; in consultation with her GP she decided to take a couple of weeks off work while she confronted long overdue issues. In writing she became aware that she was much more like a frightened 11-year-old child than an adult. Angela wrote a dialogue between the 11-year-old self and adult self. Despite this she made no headway in convincing the '11-year-old' that she was not responsible for all the behaviours of her parents. The best she could do was to tell the 11-year-old that it was not important to feel that she was not guilty, but should simply accept that half the responsibility pie for what went wrong was her father's and the other half was her mother's, with no slice for herself. Angela then changed the form of her writing to letters addressed to her parents which she did not post. Curiously when she reread the letters she noticed an absence of anger towards her parents.

Rereading the story of the trauma at a special time

You may have no one that you feel you can dictate the trauma to and you may find the prospect of writing about it yourself too daunting. However, most victims of extreme trauma usually have a typewritten account of the incident and its effects that they have given to their solicitor, police or Criminal Injury Compensation Authority (CICA). Photocopying this and rereading it at a special time can put you in charge of the memory. In your special time you might need to gradually add in a few extra details to make sure it covers all the material in Table 1.2 of Chapter 1. For example it is important to make sure the account includes details of the worst moment and it also covers how you have been affected. But the statement provides a ready-made foundation for elaborating on this chapter of your autobiography. Nevertheless it is likely that the prospect of reading it, much less editing it, fills you with dread but at least you do know you can read it because you had to read it to sign it.

The first step is to rate how bad it was on a *subjective units of distress* (SUDS) scale 0–10 (where 10 is absolutely awful) at first reading, e.g. 8 and then continue to reread or edit the statement until the SUDS score comes down by about half, e.g. to 4. The score at first reading will tend to vary from day to day and will reflect to some extent your frame of mind on that day, your general mood. After a week or two of daily reading the initial score will probably show a significant reduction from say a 9 to say a 7. There is a temptation to skim over the emotionally difficult bits of the story: this is rather like running away from the bully. To help prevent this, read each phrase or sentence twice as you go along at a slightly slower than normal reading pace for you.

In deliberately rereading the statement and editing it, you are teaching yourself that in fact nothing catastrophic happens when you objectively focus on the traumatic material. At an intellectual level, with your head you already knew this but the signal from your guts at the mere mention of the trauma is that something horrendous is going to happen if you 'go there'. The situation is not unlike having a fear of heights or vertigo: one way of dealing with this is to go to a multistorey car park, stand at the perimeter wall and test out whether you in fact fall. The person with vertigo knows that they will not fall but this information does not reach the parts that matter: the only way their guts can learn is to do it and see that nothing happens. Then they repeat going to the perimeter wall so that there is repeated disconfirmation of their negative predictions. In a similar way you can disconfirm your negative predictions of dealing with traumatic material by a rereading and editing of your statement.

Kevin was prompted to look at the statement he gave to the police after he was assaulted by a request from them to attend an identity parade. On reading his statement he was surprised that it contained no mention of seeing the fist of one of his assailants as he lay on the ground and it had the word 'HATE' tattooed across the fingers. He had remembered this only some weeks later and it hadn't occurred to him that he had not informed the police of this. (Traumatic memory is often fragmented with, as it were, bits of the jigsaw missing, which may or may not be remembered later.) He read his statement over a few times each day for a couple of days before the identity parade and his distress reduced on first readings reduced from a 10 to an 8. Unfortunately he was not able to identify anyone at the parade. He was frustrated at this and was worried that this would become yet another aspect of the trauma that he would agonise about endlessly. Kevin resolved that he would not spend the rest of his life thinking of the assault and its consequences and decided that he would give the matter his undivided attention only when he reread his statement, acknowledging it when it came up at other times but postponing it for proper consideration when he did his reading and amending of his statement at a special time. By the third week of rereading his edited statement, he was finding that he was not so much upset by it as bored by it and his nightmares were becoming less frequent.

Karen reviewed her statement in preparation for giving evidence against her rapist in court. She was struck by what she had left out, the 'weird' bits, feeling that she was looking down at herself watching herself being raped. Also she had been too embarrassed to mention that, although it certainly was not consensual sex, she had been sexually aroused at one stage. These omissions troubled her and she decided to take up a policewoman's suggestion that she might benefit from talking to staff at a local Rape Crisis Centre. At the centre a member of staff explained that often a rape was too much to take in all at once and the mind slowed the whole process down by a process of dissociation – being a spectator to begin with. Further she was told that her physiological reactions during the rape were entirely normal: 'If you press certain

buttons, certain things happen'. This did not at all imply con-
sent. Subsequently her reading of her statement evoked a
SUDS of on average 8 rather than the 10 hitherto. But her
mood even before the rape had always been subject to abrupt
fluctuations, usually for reasons she found impossible to pin
down: before the PTSD she had been diagnosed as having dysthymic disorder. Curiously she now found that on some days
when she started reading her statement her score was an 8
but occasionally it could start off as low as a 6. (Like Kevin, she
had discovered her distress at reading her statement was not
entirely due to the contents of the statement itself; the memory of the trauma was in fact an emotional memory fuelled in
part by her current emotional state.) In reading her statement
Karen questioned the wisdom of constantly replaying the video
of the rape at other times, and realised that she thought if she
played it just one more time, she would find the way it could
have all been different, a fairy story, but then she had always
liked fairy stories! It would take her some weaning off, she
concluded. Most of her relationships began as fairy stories and
turned into nightmares. Karen decided to try to view the
'video' as an old black and white movie whose content she
would examine in objective mode only at the time she allocated for the rereading of the statement. In particular 'ifs' (e.g.
'If I had gone another way home it wouldn't have happened')
were to be allocated attention only at the time she did her
rereading.

Ian reread his statement at his solicitor's suggestion following
an award from the Criminal Injuries Compensation Authority,
which was substantially less than he had hoped for. At the time
of originally making his statement, he had been hopeful that
he would get a job via a friend at a bus company and that he
would be able to drive automatic buses with his good leg: he
would be away from the club scene in which the shooting happened. Unfortunately he learnt that the Occupational Health
Department insisted that for health and safety reasons, a driver
must be able to speedily get out of his cab, which necessitated
two good legs. For his appeal against the CICA award he
needed to revise his statement to make it clear that his chances
of working again were virtually zero. His original statement did

(he thought) convey the horror of the shooting but not the effect on his long-term functioning, although his GP had confirmed that he was suffering from chronic PTSD made worse by the pain that he was often in. In rereading his statement, Ian pondered that he was probably his own worst enemy, in that he always had a joke for everyone and was always smiling, trying to make light of his pain. In particular, he wondered whether his demeanour had misled his GP and the medico-legal expert witnesses that he had seen. He was incensed that he had been videoed, which he saw as an invasion of privacy, and questions were raised about the honesty of his reported incapacity. After days of rereading his statement and editing it, it dawned on him that no money could ever replace what he had been through and he began to see the shooting as a horrible event that belonged to the past and that in the past it must remain. Ian determined that he would address it only when there was a purpose such as his CICA appeal.

Writing about it and its consequences at a special time

Treatments have been equally effective whether the person writes a page a day about the trauma and its effects, or listens to an audio-tape of their trauma. Writing about your concerns has been found to have health benefits but only if the narrative is concrete and specific. If you write in a vague, abstract, intellectual way, it can actually result in a worse outcome. There is an understandable temptation that on first writing about an extreme trauma and its effects, you might skirt around some details in order not to overwhelm yourself. However, there is a need to rapidly focus on the nitty-gritty, the sights, sounds, smells and meaning of your traumatic experience. It seems likely that it is the zooming in on these details (what is termed *referential activity*) that enables the brain to make a 'photocopy' of the trauma and operate on this. The body state that goes with the photocopy is an emotionally very dilute version of that originally triggered by remembrance of the trauma. The 'photocopy' is an 'as if' body loop, and it is much less distressing if the body begins to operate on this rather than the brain's original map of distress in the body following the extreme trauma.

Writing as if you were telling a particular chosen person about what happened to you and incorporating their imagined response tends to produce a more comprehensive account and is also likely to produce greater feelings of safety. It is possible to take further steps to avoid the spectre of being overwhelmed by writing, just very briefly to begin with, and it might take you days to write a comprehensive account. Usually it is necessary to write a page a day daily for two or three weeks to make the adequate photocopy.

Cecilia had always kept a daily journal before the road traffic accident and viewed it as her 'therapy', a way in which she got her bearings in life. In the eighteen months since her accident, she had hardly touched her journal and when she did there was no detail, it was more like a diary, a typical entry read, 'nightmare last night, *!@?~%£ accident'. She reasoned that if a journal helped with the normal hassles of life, it might also be of help over her car accident if she put in a similar amount of effort. Cecilia began her accident journal very gingerly and outlined the accident much as she had done a year earlier to her solicitor. To her annoyance she burst into tears as she had done in the solicitor's office and berated herself that she was no further on. This in turn reminded her of her daughter Amanda's crying over her homework after the accident. Her response to Amanda was to ignore the crying and to encourage her to do the homework in small chunks with lots of breaks. It took a couple of weeks but this approach worked. Cecilia decided to take her own advice, ignore the tears and write in small doses. In her writing Cecilia was surprised at how often she wrote, 'If anything had happened to the girls I couldn't have coped'. She pondered whether she was actually disturbed more by a fantasy than by the facts of the matter. For the first few days she was more conscious of the accident and her sleep worsened. Cecilia thought that the disturbed sleep might be because she was writing at her only quiet time of the day after her children went to bed, which was unfortunately just before she went to bed. She resolved to ask Amanda to clear away and wash the tea dishes while she did her homework, i.e. her journal. Afterwards she would change gear by playing briefly with Abigail and getting her ready for bed.

Peter found that memories of tending his dying colleague were more vivid when he returned to work. If he was speaking to colleagues, he could distract himself, but when he needed to concentrate to write a report he would feel compelled to look at the scaffolding and the memories would come flooding back. As a result his productivity was poor and his boss was critical of him. Much of his report writing was about colleagues' complaints and discipline matters. As he went about the building sites, he was often interrupted by a colleague asking or complaining about various matters. Over the years he had developed the habit of giving a stock reply of, 'I'll get back to you on that'. This he felt bought him time and he would sort out the various issues at a special time and then be able to give a considered response. The flashbacks and stomach turning and dropping were he reasoned very like these interruptions. It helped a little to tell himself he had done all he could but he was either getting embroiled in the intrusions or trying to dismiss them in a verbally abusive manner: both represented poor management. He resolved to note the content of the intrusions and additionally politely tell them he would sort out the material in a special report he would write after work in the early evening. Unfortunately and uncharacteristically, when the time came to write what he tried to regard as an 'incident report' he froze. Peter felt a bundle of emotions when he came to write, horror at the feel of his colleague's crushed skull in his hand, despair at the waste of a life, feelings of total inadequacy. Instead of writing he ruminated on how the man's young wife and baby would be coping, and the anguish of his father, who would probably be around his own age. Then as a practising Christian he visualised himself handing over all these emotions to Christ, his sharing the burden and weeping with him as he did over the death of his friend Lazarus. After a few days of doing this, he began to write a couple of sentences each day. He noticed how sanitised his written account was: no mention, for example, that the blood seemed to have spread everywhere and that he was surprised at how sticky it was. Over the second week he included more of the graphic detail. By the third week he found he was writing more about the effects of the incident. His difficulty now was in being under scaffolding when there was lots of activity and his lack of interest in doing anything about his financial affairs: he was annoying his wife by telling her, 'There are no pockets in a shroud'.

Patrick was on a ladder on the roof of a house, the ladder slipped and he fell about 20 feet, injuring his back, neck and legs. His ongoing pain reminded him of the excruciating pain he was in at the time of the fall: although he did not dwell on the incident, he was increasingly preoccupied with the consequences. In the first eighteen months he had been hopeful of an improvement in his physical state but unfortunately the improvement was marginal and he had become preoccupied with thoughts of worthlessness. His GP diagnosed depression and suggested he needed to accept his disability, which angered Patrick. He was however curious as to how others coped with their new self and when he heard Simon Weston (disfigured in the Falklands conflict) on radio, following publication of the second volume of his autobiography, he thought it might be therapeutic for him to also write about the impact of his trauma. As he wrote, he became very conscious of how he had isolated himself and that he always had 'good excuses', e.g. the difficulty of going uphill to the football ground of his favourite team, or the fear of being jostled in the crowd. He noted that his feelings of isolation were heightened by the guilt he felt that he was letting his wife down. Previously they enjoyed hill walking, which was now impossible, and sex had become nonexistent because of the pain involved.

By the third week of writing, much of what he had written earlier seemed more negative than was necessary, e.g. he could go to the football match but he would have to give himself more time to get there. Attendances at his local team were not so great that it was likely he would be jostled, but he had a concern about whether he could sit for forty-five minutes without being too uncomfortable and he might have to alternatively sit and stand in the aisle.

7

Restoring relationships

The focus of Chapters 5 and 6 has been on how to restore the internal workings of the body after trauma, by resetting the alarm and skilful handling of the traumatic memory. But such internal workings do not exist in a vacuum: they are affected or 'fed' by the context in which we live, our relationships, mood, whether we are in pain, how well we have slept and whether we are suffering from other disorders. In this chapter the first of these contextual factors, relationships, is addressed and the other factors are dealt with in their respective chapters: mood (Chapter 8), pain and sleep (Chapter 9) and additional disorders (Chapter 11). In a sense the purpose of these chapters is to help the reader 'starve' the traumatic memory of sustenance.

If you were injected with a drug that made you uncharacteristically irritable and emotionally numb (unable to have warm feelings for those closest to you), before too long relationships would deteriorate. This is in effect the lot of sufferers from post-traumatic stress disorder. In Chapter 2 PTSD sufferers were described as increasingly living their lives in a 'bubble', with others regarded as not part of the same story, albeit that those who have been through the same trauma can be given credence.

There is an understandable logic in estrangement from others if the trauma is interpersonal, such as assault or torture, but the same feelings of being distant and cut-off from others can arise in response to other traumas such as road traffic accidents. A trauma victim's difficulties in connecting to others may not be confined to the inner circle of close friends or family, but often extends to everyday social encounters with the development of social anxiety or phobia.

Reinvesting

A common consequence of extreme trauma is that the affected individual stops investing time and energy in others. Relationships are then viewed as 'unprofitable' and an irritant, resulting in increasing isolation. The tolerance of friends and family is strained and they may react by distancing themselves, enhancing the victim's sense of isolation still further.

Cecilia's marriage had become very strained since the car accident. Her husband, Dave, coped with what he termed her 'moodiness' by getting more involved in his hobby of diving. As a policeman he worked unsocial hours and with time off devoted to diving or taking his daughters out, they spent little time together. Cecilia had noted that they were drifting apart but was initially relieved they had little time together. She had never been entirely happy about Dave being a policeman and following the accident, she had begun ringing him at work to check that he was 'OK' and to determine when he would be home. If he was vague about when he would arrive home or arrive home late, she would get very angry. Dave in turn became angry because he felt that he was not being trusted and this was fuelled further by Cecilia's sarcastic retort, 'Bobbies are that trustworthy are they?', a reference to her longstanding belief that policemen had a particular propensity for unfaithfulness. Cecilia realised that they could not go on drifting apart and arranged for them all to go on holiday to Australia to see relatives. Dave was pleased as there were good diving facilities nearby. However, the holiday did not get off to a good start, as she had concealed from Dave that since the accident she was anxious about flying. At the airport her agitation was very apparent and Dave got angry with her for the 'idiocy' of planning such a long-haul flight if she was so anxious. She felt hurt and began crying, at which 6-year-old Abigail began crying and 14-year-old Amanda stormed off in embarrassment.

Once in Australia, Cecilia was pleased to see her cousin and to her surprise enjoyed talking about the good times in their childhood together, some of which she had quite forgotten. She recorded these early positive memories in her journal, which made her more aware that the 'chapters' she had written about the accident were not the whole story and she was not going to be dominated by them. Cecilia resolved not to have any conflicts on holiday and, though intensely irritated by her cousin's 'know-it-all' husband, did not say anything. Years previously she had coped with him using humour but did not feel able to do so now. Cecilia did not protest when Dave spent four days of the two-week holiday diving, although she was upset about his 'obsession' with diving and still resentful when they returned home.

Cecilia had realised that she needed to invest in life, and her marriage in particular, if there was to be any return but the return was very modest because of the poor quality of communication.

Kevin had become a recluse since being assaulted and resolved to resume going with his brother and three friends for their Friday night drink at a local pub. However, he was not best pleased when one of his friends greeted him with 'How is your claim going? Lay it on thick'. Kevin's stunned reaction caused his friend to change tack, but dig a yet deeper hole with 'still skiving from work'. His two other friends diverted the conversation to other matters and though they were very pleasant, Kevin was preoccupied with the initial comments. Instead of joining in, he brooded on how many people believed he was just shirking work and how little people understood him if they thought that the compensation was about money. He had moments when he made a concerted effort to join in, but he could think of nothing interesting to say: every day was the same and so he had no new experiences to report. To his brother's annoyance he made an excuse to leave the gathering early. His brother visited him the next day and Kevin told him that people just think he was 'a waste of space' for not working. Then Kevin became irritated when his brother asked him if he had been to the bank yet about the credit card he had inadvertently snapped. Kevin made a half-hearted attempt to defend himself on the basis that he had been too busy, but knew that the truth of the matter was that he no longer had the confidence to meet and explain himself to a stranger. In a shop recently he had become flustered at the checkout when the barcode on an item he purchased did not respond, and the assistant asked him whether he knew how much it was and he replied that he didn't know. Then she asked him whereabouts in the shop the item had been, his mind went totally blank and to the assistant's amazement he insisted on leaving the shop without it. At home he ruminated that the staff at the shop must think he was an idiot.

Communication Guidelines

If you meet someone from a very different background, you both make a particular effort to be very explicit about your experiences. It is as if the victim of extreme trauma and the rest of the population come from different lands with opportunities for misunderstanding ripe – in the cases described above, communication between Cecilia and her husband was non-existent and Kevin and one of his friends totally failed to connect in the pub. Matters would have been much better had they observed the Communication Guidelines in Table 7.1.

Replaying the interactions of Cecilia and Kevin through the lens of the Communication Guidelines illustrates their usefulness.

Cecilia could have begun her dialogue with her husband, Dave, along the lines of 'It is great that you are looking so good with all your diving and you have invested in your fitness, but I am unhappy with the marriage, we both need to invest in it'. This would have involved an expression of her feelings and an acknowledgement of her own role in the problem (Table 7.1 steps 3 and 4). Crucially she would have demonstrated an awareness that, for any criticism to be taken on board, her husband would first have to be positively acknowledged (Table 7.1 step 1). In so doing Cecilia would be recognising that her certainty that her criticisms were valid was no guarantee that they would be received – she needed to appreciate that 'just being

Table 7.1 **Communication Guidelines**

---

1 In stating a problem, always begin with something positive
2 Be specific
3 Express your feelings
4 Admit to your role in the problem
5 Be brief when defining problems
6 Discuss only one problem at a time
7 Summarise what your partner has said and check with them that you have correctly understood them before making your reply
8 Don't jump to conclusions, avoid mind reading, talk only about what you can see
9 Be neutral rather than negative
10 Focus on solutions
11 Behavioural change should include give and take and compromise

---

Note: Any changes agreed should be very specific.

right' was only a part of communicating her point. Emotional intelligence (Goleman 1996) refers to the ability to put yourself in other people's shoes and to appreciate what your own emotions are about. While Cecilia had a high IQ, her emotional intelligence was low – a not uncommon scenario (it is also possible to have high emotional intelligence but for this not to be matched by high IQ). Fortunately for Cecilia, unlike for IQ, it is possible to improve emotional intelligence scores by empathy awareness exercises. Cecilia had a wide range of problems including driving, marriage and her elder daughter; for her communication could be easily marred by flitting from one problem to the next like a butterfly (a violation of Table 7.1 step 5) so that no one problem was ever fully resolved in her dialogue or more accurately monologues with her long-suffering husband, Dave. She needed to focus on only one problem at a time in her dialogues (Table 7.1 step 6) to make progress, and in a sense she did this in targeting the marriage but she was not very specific (violation of Table 7.1 step 2) about which aspect of the marriage she was trying to address by arranging the family holiday in Australia: was it time for them as a couple, their sexual relationship or simply listening to each other? She had not asked Dave what he wanted to do to improve the marriage but had assumed that he was 'really only interested in diving and the kids' (a violation of Table 7.1 step 8). If she had asked him, she certainly would not have sought to clarify what he said: 'So what you are saying Dave is . . . have I got that right?' before continuing her monologue (a violation of Table 7.1 step 7).

Cecilia's frame of mind since the accident was combative and led to a negativity in dialogue with Dave rather than a neutrality as he protested, 'My ideas are shot down in flames not just disagreed with' (a violation of Table 7.1 step 9). Rather than consider a range of solutions for her marriage difficulties, Cecilia had prematurely gone for the first one that had occurred to her – the trip to Australia. If she had paused long enough to generate a menu of options, she might have come up with more viable ones such as a holiday in Scotland, which would mean a much shorter flight (a violation of Table 7.1 step 10). Finally Cecilia had fallen foul of Table 7.1 step 11: she gave her husband Dave no opportunity to help arrive at compromise solutions with regard to air travel or the duration of his diving, rather she had assumed 'deep down he does not really care' (violation of Table 7.1 step 8).

The Communication Guidelines can be used by couples on a daily basis, spending just twenty minutes a day dialoguing on a particular problem, with each partner taking it in turn to select a problem. It is best to start with the less emotionally charged problems moving onto the gradually more difficult ones as the days go by. Having a twenty-minute time limit is useful as couples tend to wander off the elected problem after this time (step 6 is the most often violated step in Table 7.1). Each partner points out when they believe one of the guidelines is being broken, akin to a yellow card being shown in a football game for a foul. If a problem is not resolved in the twenty minutes, it is left to be addressed on another day. 'Picking' at the issue at other times is forbidden; the matter is left for sharply focused attention at the special dialogue time. The procedure then helps to leave space for reinvesting and the creation of shared positive experiences. In Cecilia's case, on holiday in Australia, she could have asked Dave to play badminton with her as they had done before the accident.

The Communication Guidelines were developed with couples in mind but the framework (though probably not the daily dialogue) can be used as a 'highway code' for all trauma victims in their social interactions with those close to them. For example Cecilia could have used the Guidelines in her interaction with her daughter Amanda over leaving her muddy shoes behind the door. Simply by saying, 'It's great to see you, but do you mind cleaning your shoes and putting them in the cupboard. I know I am a bit of a fuss-pot, but if you could do it before tea that would be great', she would have complied with the first six steps of the Guidelines.

Social anxiety

The deficits in emotional intelligence exhibited by sufferers from post-traumatic stress can be manifest across the social spectrum from family, friends and colleagues to strangers. Avoidance of others is as much a hallmark of post-traumatic stress as avoidance of reminders of the trauma. Both facets of avoidance are tackled by gradual approach to what is feared.

Kevin made a start on overcoming his social avoidance by resuming meeting his friends and brother in a pub but found it an ordeal. Since his assault he was also avoiding contact with strangers. Kevin's social anxiety was so pervasive that he not only met diagnostic criteria for PTSD but also for social phobia.

In DSM-IV-TR (American Psychiatric Association 2000) social phobia is defined as

A marked and persistent fear of one or more social and performance situations in which the person is exposed to unfamiliar people or to possible scrutiny by others. The individual fears that he or she will act in a way (or show anxiety symptoms) that will he humiliating or embarrassing.

One of the key biological features of PTSD is a hypersensitive alarm (amygdala); in social phobia false alarms somehow come to be triggered by the sight or sound of other people or even by remembering or imagining oneself in the presence or thoughts of other people. Sufferers from social phobia feel that they are under a spotlight.

Kevin felt that in social situations it was as if he was at the centre of a circle; others were on the perimeter and were like teachers marking him out of ten as a human being on the basis of his social performance. Further it mattered not whether the others were strangers or friends. He could understand his fear-fulness with strangers to some extent because of his assault by a group of strangers but to feel similarly with family and friends he found incomprehensible.

When Kevin tried to justify why he had not been to the bank over his cracked credit card, his brother made a sarcastic comment, 'Who would be bothered focusing on you?' Though irritated at the time, Kevin pondered this and concluded that as he very rarely marked people out of ten as human beings on the basis of their social skills, it was indeed unlikely that they were bothering to evaluate him. He reasoned that he was not at the centre of a circle, others could not be bothered evaluat-ing him, though they might notice him in passing as just one person on the edge of the circle like everybody else. Kevin also noticed that some of the people he liked most were not par-ticularly socially skilful; indeed the most skilful people were probably politicians and who likes a politician!

Anger

The development of uncharacteristic irritability is a common consequence of extreme trauma and is one of the diagnostic symptoms for PTSD in DSM-IV-TR (American Psychiatric Association 2000). Such anger can easily sabotage relation-ships. However, anger should not be regarded as necessarily negative. Anger can convey that there has been an injustice and it is doubtful whether injustices such as apartheid in South Africa would ever have been corrected without the 'head of steam' generated by this emotion.

At an individual level Bob, who had been bullied at work and suffered prolonged duress stress disorder (PDSD) as a consequence, came from a family background that 'didn't do anger'. Had he displayed anger to his boss, the likelihood is that he would not have developed PDSD. His PDSD began to resolve when he got angry about his boss and focused this energy on pursuing litigation against his employer. In many ways anger is rather like a laser: sharply focused it has enormous power for good, but for most trauma victims their new-found anger is destructive.

Many trauma victims have an ongoing sense of threat and vulnerability. In Chapter 2 it was explained that this relates primarily to the operation of the brain's amygdala (alarm) and that the setting has become such that the person feels as if they are in a 'war zone'. Unsurprisingly faced with this level of 'threat', there is a desire to totally control everything, but unfortunately normal life is not neat and tidy, things do not run completely to plan and consequently there is outrage over very minor hassles. The uncharacteristic irritability can be construed as an attempt to compensate for being out of control in the trauma and to manage the perceived high level of ongoing threat. It is as if the mind says, 'If I just have everything ordered then I will be able to stop terrible things happening'. This is a regression to the magical thinking of the young child, e.g. 'If I don't step on the cracks in the pavement on the way to school then teacher will not shout at me'. In PTSD the amygdala has hijacked mental processing creating a background emotion of threat and vulnerability which in turn contributes to the appraisal of hassles as catastrophes. It is therefore necessary to learn to separate out what proportion of an emotional reaction is due to the background emotion and what proportion is actually due to events of today.

Pedro had PTSD and a great deal of anger towards his father, who had abused his mother, but he also got angry at himself for, as a child, tackling his father and the latter leaving home. His ruminations about the events led to an irritability that soured his marriage and his relationships with his children. He decided to focus his anger by writing a letter to his father that he would not post, refusing to get hooked by the anger at other times. Pedro viewed the anger as bait that he would not rise to but would address the material of the bait including his self-blame at the special time.

Sam was irritable at home and at work following his road traffic accident and his boss had reprimanded him for needlessly upsetting one of the secretaries. His boss had had to persuade the secretary not to initiate a formal grievance procedure against Sam and he had admonished him with 'For God's sake stop and think before you open your mouth'. Driving home that night Sam was fuming at the indignity of being reprimanded yet again when he stopped at a set of traffic lights and realised that he needed to utilise 'lights' for his anger. When he got home he refined the lights strategy further: at the first signs of anger he would imagine a set of traffic lights on red and shout 'Stop' to himself, as the lights went to amber he would ask himself, 'Did he/she really do that deliberately to wind me up? Is what he/she has done really the end of the world?' And when the lights went to green he would go off somewhere else to calm down.

To his surprise he managed to successfully apply the strategy when one of his children protested that it was too early for her to go to bed. However, later his wife Maria got angry with him when he told her he had been reprimanded at work and he applied the traffic light routine again, this time by walking out of the house. Sam felt he had done well and calmed down soon into his walk, but on returning home his wife was furious that he had 'abandoned' her. He explained to her the routine he had been applying and gradually she became calm and suggested that on green, Sam could just walk to another room briefly to compose himself but not leave the house, and he agreed to this. Encouraged by his success at home, Sam decided to apply the strategy at work and found that sometimes he was more able to do it than at other times. His difficulty was that sometimes he simply did not think 'traffic lights', so he decided to employ a reminder: a red dot on one knuckle, a yellow one on the adjacent knuckle and a green dot on the next. The 'lights' were more apparent when he made a fist in anger. When he explained this strategy to his wife, Maria jokingly said that perhaps she and the children should put similar dots on their forehead, a strategy enthusiastically received by his 7-year-old daughter. Maria then suggested they might use a 'traffic light' coloured air freshener in the car and have one or two at home as well. Listening to the conversation his daughter told him that she would tell him when he was being a 'growly bear' and Sam agreed to contort his face as much as possible at this cue. In this way he used the emotions associated with humour to replace the emotion of anger 'mood over mood'.

8

Managing mood

The memory of your trauma is an emotional memory in that it is likely to be vividly recalled if you are upset for any reason, even if it is totally unconnected with the trauma. Thus the better you become at managing your mood, the less likely it is that you will access the traumatic material and the accompanying sights, sounds and smells of the trauma.

How we think about something has a critical effect on how we feel. If a neighbour walks past you without acknowledging you, you may think that he/she has a lot on their mind or you might think they are deliberately snubbing you; the former will produce little emotional arousal while the latter might evoke anger. It is as if we take photographs of situations from our own particular angle, using our own lenses and unique camera settings. A key feature of cognitive therapy is to teach clients to stand back from what has upset them and assess whether it would be more appropriate to look at the situation from a different angle.

Depressed mood may arise as a consequence of a series of minor events or hassles, none of which by themselves seem of great significance leading to a depression about depression. The path to this double dose of depression involves first a minor hassle that has been overreacted to, the resulting distress impairs coping with the next hassle which in turn can lead to self-blame for not handling trivia properly. The scene is then set for inadequate coping with successive irritations. Thus by the end of a day filled with the normal hassles of life an individual can feel not only very low but also annoyed with themselves for their distress. This in turn will increase the frequency and intensity of traumatic memories which will likely also affect sleep. To interrupt the cumulative effect of hassles it is therefore necessary to filter each so that the negative impact of one is dissipated before the next.

On second thoughts

The thought record in Table 8.1 is a very effective filter that can be interposed between hassles to interrupt their cumulative effect. The thought record can be used to help take a better 'picture' of what is upsetting you. 'MOOD' is a mnemonic for remembering the mood-altering framework in Table 8.1. The first letter 'M' stands for monitoring mood: 'What am I feeling? What mood am I in?' and 'What effect is it having on others?' Noticing and understanding the origins of dips in mood is a key aspect of emotional intelligence; without this it is not possible to fine tune emotions as you

Table 8.1 **MOOD management**

Monitor mood	Observe thinking	Objective thinking	Decide what to do and do it

go along so that by the time you are forced to recognise the distress it is much more difficult to do anything about it. The first 'O' stands for observing your thinking or images, identified by asking, 'What have I been saying to myself to feel the way I do?' The second 'O' stands for objective thinking – a standing back from an upset and having second thoughts. The second thoughts can be distilled by asking, 'How true is it? How useful is this way of thinking? Would others be looking at this in a different way?' The 'D' stands for deciding to put into practice the more objective way of thinking. The final column is an antidote to agonising or ruminating about what is upsetting and is a rallying cry to action.

Completing the first column can be more problematic than it first appears, as in some instances you may identify a specific thought; but sometimes the thoughts that are causing problems are more at the edge of awareness in the form of a daydream and are just as relevant. The procedure for identifying these more insidious thoughts can be likened to watching a slow motion action replay of a goal in a football game in order to properly see how the ball got in the back of the net.

John was concerned about the 'weird' aspects of the gas explosion: he had found it strange that the ball of flame had come towards him as if in slow motion but soon afterward was able to dismiss it as peculiar to the extreme experience. From time to time he had the experience of watching himself as if through a window and this distressed him. Using the framework of Table 8.1, John's mood was lowered by this experience (dissociation), his observed thinking was 'I am going mad', and his objective thinking became 'Does it matter that I am sometimes a spectator to myself for a few minutes any more than it was weird seeing the ball of flame coming towards me?' He decided that when he had this experience he would (final column) note it but refuse to dwell on it and tune all his senses into something else, e.g. looking at the glistening raindrops on leaves in the garden, the smell of the freshly cut grass.

John's mood was also lowered by his emotional numbness: he felt flat and guilty that since the explosion he did not feel warm to his wife and had no libido. He also felt a mixture of jealousy and anger when his closest friend and colleague Alan (who was also involved in the explosion) visited and there was banter between Alan and his wife. John sometimes pondered whether Alan and his wife were having an affair. He interrupted his endless agonising to complete the MOOD thought record in Table 8.2.

John went for the pub lunch with his wife and Alan but during it they reminisced that initially management had tried to blame them for the explosion. At home afterwards John began to dwell on the comment of his foreman, 'You must have done something wrong' and stopped himself stewing on this by again using the Mood record. In the final column John had used humour to better manage his anger. It should be noted

Table 8.2 John's MOOD thought record

Monitor mood	**O**bserve thinking	**O**bjective thinking	**D**ecide what to do and do it
Irritated, sad, wife has just told me Alan is calling in at lunchtime.	They're having an affair, don't blame her the way I've been. Bloody Alan, should have died in the explosion.	He's hardly likely to be having an affair with the burns and pain he has, poor guy. I banter with his wife and it doesn't mean anything.	I will make it special for wife and Alan, suggest we all go out for a pub lunch when he arrives. It is what I do that is important not what I feel.
Angry at employers.	Ungrateful bosses, why blame me after all I had done for them.	They blamed Alan as well. It is just what organisations do, dump you as soon as you are not convenient.	They are not worth my attention, just imagine foreman sitting constipated on the toilet.

that if John had not completed his thought record first of all with regard to the 'affair', then he would likely have been too debilitated to properly handle thoughts of the unfairness of his employer and his mood would have begun spiralling downwards.

Stepping around biases in thinking

The focus in a thought record is on the content of observed thinking (Table 8.1 column 2). If Table 8.1 is completed in response to many upsetting situations, though the content of thinking may differ, they can be linked by the same underlying thought processes. For example inspection of John's thought records indicate a tendency to personalise matters – in that he sees both his wife's supposed errant behaviour and that of his bosses as attributable to himself. Personalisation is just one of ten possible biases in information processing (Table 8.3) that can sabotage the handling of hassles and negative life events.

Peter felt very guilty that he had not known what to do when his colleague fell from scaffolding and was troubled by the thought that maybe if he had put him in the right position instead of cradling him in his arms, he would have survived. The guilt feelings haunted him and he felt too ashamed to tell anyone. Peter was using emotional reasoning (Table 8.3 bias 7) and concluding that because he felt guilty, he must be. Trauma-related guilt is a common consequence of enduring a trauma in which others have died, but it is a bogus guilt in that there is no known alternative way of handling the situation. One day Peter's wife arrived home upset, not an uncommon experience after she had visited her mother. He asked her what the 'dragon' had done now and she replied, 'Just hug me'; as he hugged her he reflected that this was probably what his colleague had wanted most. Later he told his wife about the guilt feelings and she pointed out that he had stayed with his colleague long after he could have gone off and just being there was important. But Peter initially brushed this aside, saying, 'I only did what any human being would do', an example of automatic discounting (Table 8.3 bias 4) but she

Table 8.3 **Biases in information processing**

---

1 *Dichotomous thinking:* everything is seen in black and white terms, for example, 'I am either in control of what's happening to me or I am not'.

2 *Over-generalisation:* expecting a uniform response from a category of people because of the misdeeds of a member, for example, 'All men are potential rapists'.

3 *Mental filter:* seizing on a negative fragment of the situation and dwelling on it, for example, 'I could have been killed in that encounter'.

4 *Automatic discounting:* brushing aside the positive aspects of what was achieved in a trauma, for example, 'I was only doing my duty in saving the child'.

5 *Jumping to conclusions:* assuming that it is known what others think, for example, 'They all think I should be better by now, it was six weeks ago after all'.

6 *Magnification and minimisation:* magnification of shortcomings and minimisation of strengths, for example, 'Since the trauma, I'm so irritable with the family and just about manage to keep going to work'.

7 *Emotional reasoning:* focusing on emotional state to draw conclusions about oneself, for example, 'Since it happened, I'm frightened of my own shadow, I guess I'm just a wimp'.

8 *'Should' statements:* inappropriate use of moral imperatives – 'shoulds', 'musts', 'haves', and 'oughts' – for example, 'It's ridiculous that since the attack I now have to take my daughter with me shopping. I should be able to go by myself'.

9 *Labelling and mislabelling:* exaggeratedly negative descriptions of yourself, for example, 'I used to think of myself as a strong person. I could handle anything, but since it happened I'm just weak'.

10 *Personalisation:* assuming that because something went wrong it must be your fault, for example, 'I keep going over my handling of the situation. I must have made a mistake somewhere for the child to have died'.

---

replied that neither his boss nor a colleague from Human Resources had stayed. She suggested seeing the 'guilt' was just like a 'cold', a nuisance that he should ignore and which would fade of its own accord.

Kevin blamed himself for walking alone in the city centre at 2 a.m. before his assault; he thought of himself as having been stupid and confided his 'stupidity' to his brother, who responded, 'So am I stupid for walking alone in town, getting a taxi home last weekend after a night out?' Kevin replied, 'You were taking a chance', but his brother insisted in his lawyer-like way, 'Was I stupid?' Kevin could not bring himself to say that his brother had been stupid and afterwards reflected on whether he could have one law for others, 'They are allowed to take reasonable risks', and another for himself. He decided not to take his guilt feelings seriously but was still troubled by the thought, 'I should have known'. The more he thought about it, the more he realised this 'should' (Table 8.3 bias 8) was entirely inappropriate; he reflected that he never did have a crystal ball. Kevin was still concerned about his repeated checking, which was having more serious consequences since he had finally returned to work. In the morning, before leaving home, he was repeatedly checking that he had switched off appliances and locked his door, and to such an extent that he was arriving at work late. His assistant at work was becoming increasingly irritated with him because he insisted on checking her work before she liaised with the public. Matters came to a head when in an angry outburst she called him a 'control freak'. Kevin was upset by this as he had had a good relationship with her prior to the assault. Musing on this, he recalled how out of control he had felt when assaulted and his stomach turned at the memory. But in an attempt never to experience these emotions again, he had gone to the opposite extreme of trying to control everything. He reasoned that it was his 'black and white thinking' (dichotomous thinking: Table 8.3 bias 1), 'I am either in control or out of control', that was causing his problems and that he needed to have as his goal a degree of control. This still frightened Kevin, as it meant giving up the quest for a feeling of certainty and that he would have to get used to carrying some uncertainty. He decided that he was paying too high a price for absolute certainty. However, he was relieved that the real issues were not actually about his assistant or the security of his home and he could begin to stand back from these concerns.

Karen began to automatically blame herself after she was sexually abused by her cousin in childhood but this became more pronounced a decade later when she was raped and violently assaulted by her partner. Although she had a good circle of friends and supportive parents, after meeting them she would agonise about some aspect of the encounter and then telephone them to apologise if she had upset them. Invariably they were baffled by her response and regarded it as a quaint, if slightly frustrating, idiosyncrasy. Karen's difficulties were a consequence of habitually using a mental filter (Table 8.3 bias 3) and were crystallised when she telephoned her father to see if she had upset him when she visited because he had been quiet. Her father confessed that he had been quiet because he knew a football match was on TV shortly and if he was more than monosyllabic she would chat away and he would miss the match. In his defence her father said that he had played games with the baby for thirty minutes before becoming quiet for a few minutes. Karen began to get upset on the telephone, then her father said:

> It's like you are always watching *Match of the Day* but the recorded highlight of games that you feature are always of fouls and you then think it was a 'dirty' game, but if you were actually at the match you would know it was a good game despite the fouls.

Henceforth she became aware that her reflex response was to distort her social experiences without actually lying, and that she needed to check out her gut reaction before engaging in post mortems.

Stepping around a prejudice against yourself

Many of those suffering long-term debility following an extreme trauma develop a negative view of themselves. At its mildest they may simply blame themselves for feeling the way they do and at its more severe see themselves as worthless without any redeeming qualities. Both the extremes of a negative view of self can be thought of as occupying either ends of a line.

Karen after her sexual abuse as a child was at the mild end of the line: she felt that there was something wrong with her for sometimes feeling emotionally numb and would blame herself for doing what she saw as 'daft things' and as inappropriately flirting to try to lift her mood. But it was not until the physical and sexual assaults by her baby's father that she moved to the other end of the line and regarded herself as worthless. At this end of the line it is as if the individual has developed a prejudice against themselves. This prejudice in turn leads to biases in information processing.

The prejudice model is shown in Figure 8.1: the model owes its origins to Padesky and Greenberg (1995).

You can think of the prejudice developed post trauma, e.g. 'I am flawed, fundamentally defective, haven't got what it takes any more' as having the shape on the left-hand side. Only that which fits the 'shape' of the prejudice is processed, thus anything negative (rectangular shaped), e.g. a critical comment from somebody, will be agonised over. By contrast you will be uncomfortable with anything positive (oval shaped) such as praise from someone because it does not fit and it is rejected, e.g. 'He/she is just trying to be nice and does not really mean it'. Further neutral information (the circle with the cross inside) does not fit either and it is twisted to

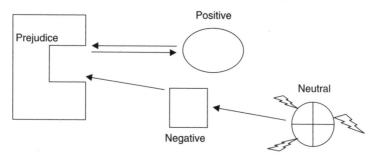

Figure 8.1 Prejudice model.

assume a rectangular shape, e.g. an innocuous comment, 'I thought you were going the hairdressers?', is met with an angry retort, 'What's wrong with my hair anyway?' The upshot of the 'prejudice' is that you have a constant diet of psychological junk food. Although you cannot stop the prejudice welling up, you can teach yourself to step around it. It is akin to having parents or grandparents who were racially or religiously prejudiced and to your embarrassment as an adult you may not be able to stop these feelings coming on-stream, but knowing their origin it is possible to act deliberately contrary to them, e.g. going out of your way to be hospitable to the 'victim' of the prejudice. As the prejudice is contradicted in action it gradually loses its force but you need to be vigilant for its unexpected appearance at a 'gut' level, e.g. finding that you are doubting your ability to do a task that you had done many times before the trauma. An ability to circumvent the 'prejudice' is a prerequisite for enabling you to access a problem-solving mode.

Sam developed a prejudice against himself following his road traffic accident. The prejudice had a number of sources: first of all he blamed himself for not having protected his children, and second, he agonised over questions such as 'If I had been paying attention more would it have happened?' and 'If I hadn't been tired would it have happened?' Sam left the questions in mid-air, never properly answering them, just 'picking' at them rather like at a sore. The effect of the prejudice was that he had lost his confidence not only for driving but also in work, in that he never instigated initiatives rather he wished to fade into the background, contenting himself with criticising others. The upshot was that he himself became the target of criticism, the square box in Figure 8.1, which fitted neatly into his prejudice against himself and he would stew endlessly on the criticism, thus reinforcing his bigotry against himself. Further if a supportive colleague pointed out that he had not taken a lead role on something he would twist this neutral comment, the circle in Figure 8.1, into a negative. Favourable comments from a supportive colleague were dismissed (the triangle in Figure 8.1) on the basis that he was just a particularly nice guy.

Bob developed a prejudice against himself from the prolonged bullying at work. Years after leaving his employment, he berated himself that he had not taken out a formal grievance against his boss and that if he had then he might not have had to give up work. His prejudice was fuelled by a belief that 'I should have known'. However, when he replayed the specifics of the incidents in work he recalled (a) he had thought that the bullying would escalate if he put in a grievance, (b) management always backs the manager and would dismiss the conflict as a 'personality clash' (c) his Occupational Health Department had arranged counselling and he had assumed they would have put at least informal pressure on management for change – in fact his manager had flown into a rage when he asked for time off for counselling, nullifying any benefits he got from it. (The psychological effects of work-related bullying are discussed in Scott and Stradling 2000.) Bob concluded that there never was a 'Bob' with the knowledge he now had and that he was blaming someone who never existed, a cardboard cut-out of himself. He decided that when he was mocking himself he would visualise all his 'hot air' blowing a hole in the cardboard cut-out of himself.

Loss of a valued role

An inevitable consequence of extreme trauma is some degree of impairment in occupational or social functioning. In some instances the person may be totally unable to perform their previous role and in others they may perceive themselves as no longer being able to play a role well enough. If the role that has been jettisoned or impaired is regarded as central to the person's identity, then the scene is set for the development of depression. However, the depression is likely to persist only if the previous role or roles were overvalued. Depression may also occur as a result of an exaggeratedly negative perception of role performance post trauma.

Patrick had worked all his life as a labourer on a building site and more recently repairing roofs. Initially he was not too dismayed by the effects of his fall from a roof, thinking he would probably be fit for work after about six months. When this milestone passed with only a slight improvement in his condition, he became steadily more despondent and was diagnosed as suffering from depression eighteen months after the fall. What upset Patrick was not only could he not do his job but also he missed no longer being called upon by relatives and friends to do practical jobs and felt 'useless'. About the time he was diagnosed with depression, his friend Paul, a former colleague and builder's labourer, became terminally ill with cancer and on one of his visits to him in the hospice, Paul asked him, 'Why am I still here?' At the time Patrick was taken aback and parried the question with a reply, 'Why, where do you think you are going?' But after the visit Paul's question haunted him: he reflected on the visit, the tenderness of Paul holding his hand, the banter between Paul's son and Paul, when the latter said he had made his peace with God. Tearfully Patrick concluded that Paul was here to make love visible and that he was a gift. He was then struck by the irony of seeing Paul on his deathbed, weak, a shadow of his former self, as a gift and himself still able to walk around and visit people as useless. Patrick realised he had not just valued his former job, he had in fact overvalued it. He was going to miss Paul and later, at his funeral, decided to 'let him get a word in edgeways' whenever he was tempted to be inactive. Paul's language on the building site had always been colourful, to say the least, and would prompt him into activity out of respect. No longer would Patrick heed the 'Old Codger' in his head telling him he is 'useless', instead he would listen to Paul. Patrick mused that precisely what anyone can or cannot do is really beside the point.

When he arrived home after Paul's funeral, Patrick's new perspective was abruptly challenged, as one of his daughters was arguing with his wife that she needed money for clothes. Patrick felt dismayed, the conflict underlined his feelings of inadequacy as a husband and father in that he was no longer able to provide for his family. Ignoring the argument he walked straight to his bedroom. His wife soon joined him and apologised that he had had to come home to such an atmosphere on such a day. Patrick insisted that she had no need to apologise and that it was he who had let the family down. However, his wife retorted that their teenage daughter was being a 'madam' and that he had had to go without as a child and it did him no harm. He reflected that he had regarded his father as a good father even though he was unemployed for most of his childhood and adolescence – he hadn't lost the role of father, he just thought he had.

Role impairment

An extreme trauma is likely to affect your performance in a number of roles. Patrick's occupational functioning was drastically affected, but the effect on his other roles, such as a husband, was less pronounced. How you think about yourself will be very much affected by the view you take of the roles you currently perform. Further you are likely to contrast your current performance with that before the trauma. If a particular role is important to you and there has been a big deterioration in performance, this 'performance gap' is likely to lower your mood. You can see your life as an unfolding drama, punctuated by the trauma. You can assess your performance using the Role Performance Questionnaire in Table 8.4.

When rating your change in performance since the trauma it is easy to forget that what you are actually rating is a perceived performance and that others might have a different view of your performance or they might have a different take on the required standard.

After her head injury, Sandra saw her performance at work as more of a problem than did colleagues. In her view her 'performance gap' (a 9 at work before her climbing accident and a 3 when she returned to work afterwards) was enormous (9–3=6), but it was much less so as far as her colleagues were concerned.

It is important to check with those on the receiving end of a particular role their perception of your performance. The observer perspective on the 'performance gap' can differ markedly from your own.

Table 8.4 **Role Performance Questionnaire**

This questionnaire is designed to help assess any changes in your ability to carry out everyday roles, e.g. as a mother, since the incident. Please indicate using a scale 0–10 (where a 10 would be performing a role superbly, 0 would be carrying out the role very badly and a 5 would be performing the role 'so-so') how well you were doing before and now. For example a score of 7 would mean you were playing a particular role pretty well, while a score of 3 would mean you were carrying out a role pretty badly. Just complete the questionnaire for the roles that apply to you. Leave blank those that do not apply. If there is a role that is not included in the list but it is important to you, e.g. grandfather, student, add this onto the list and rate your performance before the incident and currently.

Me as:	*Before the incident*	*Now*
Mother		
Father		
Daughter		
Son		
Wife		
Husband		
Partner		
Employee		
Employer		
Friend		

Irreparably damaged?

One of the casualties of an extreme trauma can be the loss of a sense of 'me'. At its mildest this might be expressed as 'I am not the same person' or more extremely as 'I am irreparably damaged'. By completing the Role Performance Questionnaire (Table 8.4) you can become aware that there are in fact multiple selves, e.g. how you are with your partner, how you are with a friend etc. While you may feel that your performance has deteriorated in many of these roles, it is probably less in some than others, and this can help to counter the wholly negative view of self that can develop post trauma. By looking at how you can improve performance in particular roles, the sense of having been irreparably damaged and the accompanying feelings of hopelessness may be diminished.

Tessa suffered from bulimia for about a year in her late teens, she had had low self-esteem ever since she could remember, and although she had a reasonable relationship with her mother, the latter doted on her two older brothers. She felt unattractive and would comfort herself by binge eating, then vomiting and engaging in excessive exercise. Her eating disorder gradually resolved when she met Bill, whom she later married and she began to think of herself as an attractive, intelligent woman. The roles of 'attractive woman' and 'intelligent person' became as much a part of her identity as 'wife', 'mother', 'daughter'. After her riding accident she felt irreparably damaged both physically and mentally. In completing the Role Performance Questionnaire, she pencilled in 'attractive woman' and 'intelligent person' in the spaces at the bottom of the column headed 'Me as'. She had never, despite Bill's help, had a great belief in her attractiveness as a woman and she rated this as having been a 7 before the riding accident, but because of the scar on her forehead and her crutches, she rated her current attractiveness as 1. The perceived performance gap of 6 (7–1) reflected her body dysmorphic disorder (an exaggeratedly negative view of a minor physical anomaly). Tessa thought that before her trauma she operated as an intelligent person and rated herself as 8 in this regard, but since her fall from the horse she regarded herself as a 'cretin' with a score of 2. In part, some of this performance gap of 6 (8–2) was attributable to the mild cognitive impairment stemming from her fall but she also had an exaggeratedly negative view of her performance. Tessa's completed Role Performance Questionnaire is shown in Table 8.5.

Tessa noticed that the change in performance in most roles was

Table 8.5 Tessa's Role Performance Questionnaire

Me as:	Before the incident	Now
Mother	8	6
Father		
Daughter	7	5
Son		
Wife	9	6
Husband		
Partner		
Employee	8	4
Employer		
Friend	8	6
Attractive woman	7	1
Intelligent person	8	2

most typically just 2 and while there were particularly problematic roles (employee, attractive woman and intelligent
person) her use of a mental filter in focusing exclusively on
these was distorting the overall picture of herself. Indeed, she
wondered whether she was not using a mental filter in focusing on the scar on her forehead and was neglecting to take into
account her positive physical attributes. This self-questioning
was prompted by a comment of her husband, Bill, as he was
watching the World Cup on TV. He asked her, 'Do you find Alan
Hansen, the football commentator attractive?' and she replied
with enthusiasm, 'Yes'. To which Bill queried, 'How come? Look
at the scar on his forehead'. At the time she felt irritated at being
trapped and snapped back, 'He's not on crutches', to which he
replied 'Would you fancy him less if he was on crutches?' She
did not reply but pondered that the scarring or disability didn't
seem to make the difference she thought it would. For a time
Tessa was able to dismiss Bill's assault on her prejudice against
herself, by telling herself that attractiveness is different for

men and women, but increasingly acknowledged that she had exaggerated this difference. She began to gradually dare herself to expose her forehead.

Tessa noticed that interviewers on TV appeared intelligent by summarising what the other person says, 'So you are saying ... are you?' She thought that if she tried it out, others would feel listened to and she would buy space to properly understand what others were thinking before making her reply. Further it was not so much what interviewers said that mattered but whether they smiled and their body language showed that they were open to what the other person said. She comforted herself with the thought that at least smiling and having an open posture when talking to people did not mean she had to think! Tessa's boss at the shop allowed her to continue to work there, but on reduced hours, and suggested she do only one task at a time rather than juggling a number of tasks as she had done before the riding accident. She found she got much less stressed operating a turnstile for tasks rather than having an open door. Tessa found that she could cope with large tasks by breaking them down to small tasks and again doing only one at a time. She tried the same approach to reading but found it was not sufficient to read just for a few minutes. However, if she made brief written notes, the information seemed to stick. Using these strategies Tessa was able to reduce her performance gap with regards to being an intelligent person. While she still felt irreparably physically damaged, she no longer felt that way as a person, albeit that she still did not feel the same person.

Broad investment portfolio

All roles pass: to be hooked on a role is to court depression. It is extremely easy to get hooked on a particular role, because the very success of the role acts as a magnet to invest further in the role to the neglect of other investments. In the wake of an extreme trauma, investment in previous roles is often problematic; the temptation is to then abandon the process of investment, but no investment means no return. The need is to develop and maintain a broad investment portfolio. This means making some speculative investments as well as considered ones, anticipating that there will be both positive and negative surprises. With a broad investment portfolio there are checks and balances offering the best prospects of a return.

Patrick was physically very limited in what he could do after his fall from a roof. Working as a roofer was impossible, with difficulty he could mow his lawn and do some maintenance tasks. His previous investments had been largely manual, but after Paul's funeral he became conscious of a need to commit to a new direction. He decided to enquire at the hospice about being a volunteer and became involved in fund-raising events. Patrick had abandoned his hobby of fishing after the accident because of his injuries, and had dwelt on how much he missed it and the 'unfairness of it all' (depressive rumination). As part of his stock-taking he became conscious of how he had developed a habit of seeing everything in extreme terms (dichotomous thinking), e.g. either his teenage daughter's behaviour was a catastrophe or, on very rare occasions, she was a saint; he could either fish as he had done previously or not fish at all. He realised that there was probably a middle way with most things and with regard to fishing he suspected he probably could manage an hour or so in a local park but that with his pain it probably would be impossible to spend several hours fishing at choice venues some distance away. Patrick had never been a reader but he decided to timetable into his week a visit to his local library. To his surprise he found himself drawn to the local history section, especially accounts of the part of his city that he knew from childhood, which had been largely redeveloped, or 'massacred' in his view. He knew from family legend that his family had moved to England from Ireland at the time of the potato famine in the 1840s and he decided to trace his ancestry back as far as he could. To his amazement, at the librarian's prompting, he found himself enrolling on a computer course to facilitate the quest for his origins.

Timetable uplifts

Probably the biggest saboteur of a viable investment portfolio is that the person waits to see how they feel before embarking on a task. In the aftermath of an extreme trauma, mood is inevitably low, resulting in inactivity and usually depression about the inactivity. Timetabling into the week potentially uplifting events acts as a protection against underinvestment. The timetable should reflect a balance of items that are designed to primarily give a sense of achievement, e.g. clearing out a room, and those which would primarily give a sense of pleasure, e.g. watching a DVD. It does mean however that in the short term there is often little to show for the investment.

Patrick began fishing in his local park and it was not until his fifth visit that he got any enjoyment from it. Up till then he had felt that he was going through the motions, albeit that in the earlier visits he had got some sense of achievement for at least doing something with his day. He had set himself a task of clearing out a spare room at home but had quickly become frustrated and angry as he embarked on this task. Fortunately, his wife suggested that he start on the box room and do one shelf, then have a break, then do another shelf and take a break. Patrick protested that it would take forever, to which she replied, 'Who is holding a gun to your head saying it has got to be done by a certain time?' He then realised he was putting pressure on himself to deliver in exactly the way he had done before the fall and had to accept that there was a limited amount of petrol in the tank now but he could make best use of it by going at an appropriate speed.

Coping self-statements

Young children often express their thoughts out loud while they are playing and gradually their utterances become an internal dialogue, it is this self-talk that then guides our actions. Donald Meichenbaum (1985) has developed Self Instruction Training (SIT), which is a crystallisation of the series of categories of self-talk that are necessary for handling stressors (see Table 8.6).

Problems such as self-consciousness following trauma (which may approach the level of body dysmorphic disorder)

Table 8.6 Self Instruction Training

1 Preparing for the stressor
2 Encountering the stressor
3 Coping with feeling overwhelmed
4 Review of coping efforts/stressor

and the effects of acquired brain injury are particularly amenable to a SIT approach.

Ian, who was shot in the leg when working as a bouncer, used a set of coping self-statements with regard to going swimming. In preparation for his visit to the pool (Table 8.6 category 1) he told himself, 'Once I am in the water no one will see the scarring on my leg'. He anticipated being very self-conscious walking from the changing room to the pool and decided to tell himself, 'People can like me or lump me, I am still me' (Table 8.6 category 2). In the event of someone staring at him or saying something, he decided he would tell himself to focus straight ahead and concentrate on his destination (Table 8.6 category 3). Afterwards he decided to review how these self-statements worked out (Table 8.6 category 4) and he told himself, 'The strategies worked well, it was uncomfortable with the stares of some teenage boys but I am not going to be bullied by them into not going'.

Sandra suffered an acquired brain injury following her fall when climbing, in which her partner was killed. After returning to work six months later, she found herself struggling to keep up at work meetings. At her cognitive behavioural therapy treatment sessions it was agreed with her therapist that in preparation for meetings she would tell herself, 'It is only a meeting: I don't have to give answers there and then as I did before the fall' (Table 8.6 category 1). Then as she anticipated her tension rising with the small talk that occurs as people assemble for the meeting, she would tell herself, 'So long as you smile at someone and show some interest in them, they are perfectly happy' (Table 8.6 category 2). At some point in the meeting she felt that the spotlight would be on her and she anticipated feeling overwhelmed. She decided that she would simply repeat the words the other person was saying and bounce it back to them: 'So you are saying . . . have I got that right?' This would give her time to think as well as making the other person feel properly listened to, but if she still did not understand, she would simply say, 'Can I get back to you on that?' (Table 8.6 category 3). Finally she would review how the strategy worked, asking herself 'Did anyone actually comment negatively? What is the actual evidence that people were negative?' (Table 8.6 category 4). In order to become familiar with this series of self-statements, her therapist got her to role-play a meeting she was due to attend. At work she was also struggling with the volume of work coming her way. Prior to her fall Sandra had prided herself on being able to juggle tasks; now by mid-afternoon she was totally exhausted and unable to work. Following discussion with her therapist, she decided that when she experienced a knot in her stomach before going to work, she would tell herself, 'I am going to operate a turnstile, one little task through at a time and then a break, what gets done gets done, I can no longer have an open door to tasks' (Table 8.6 category 1). However, on arrival at work her phone would ring and somebody would be demanding her attention. She agreed she would take a deep breath and as she slowly exhaled tell herself to 're-lax' while simultaneously relaxing any part of her body that was tense, then telling herself, 'It's a marathon: don't exceed the speed limit. One manageable task at a time followed by a break' (Table 8.6 category 2). Inevitably in the course of the day something would become very urgent and she would begin to feel overwhelmed. At this stage she agreed to tell herself:

I will put my current task to the other side of the turnstile and concentrate exclusively on the priority, breaking it down into manageable sub-tasks if necessary, with breaks in between. The length of the queue the other wide of the turnstile is not my problem. (Table 8.6 category 3)

In her review of her coping strategies she decided to remind herself of how many tasks she had actually completed in the day and of the extent to which she had been able to work a full day (Table 8.6 category 4). At her therapy session, she acknow-ledged that she was completing more and feeling less tired using the 'turnstile' and that it was much better than going home at the end of a working day with no job complete and a lot of jobs partially completed. However, she did become flustered when others demanded that she address their difficulties immediately; she found that since the fall she would lose track when trying to explain or justify her position. This in turn gave the demanding colleague ammunition that could be used against her and she would feel helpless. To circumvent this the therapist suggested that at category 3 she should keep it simple by just repeating over and over a one-liner (the broken record technique – so called because it resembles the effect of a needle stuck in the one groove of an old gramophone record) independent of what the other person says. Sandra decided that a suitable category 3 statement would be 'I will put it in the queue' and she rehearsed using this with the therapist.

The advantage of SIT for those with acquired brain injuries is that it is less cognitively demanding than the cognitive restructuring involved in say the use of the MOOD framework.

Jack's mother and the staff at his day centre helped him overcome his difficulties (anxiety disorder not otherwise specified) after he had been knocked down crossing a road, using a variation of SIT called 'stop-think-relax', pioneered by Robin Chapman and his colleagues (2006). The day centre staff introduced Jack to the use of stop-think-relax to help him manage his outbursts following the accident. On a piece of paper near the top they drew a red traffic light to indicate the need to stop at the first signs of anger. Under this they drew a picture of a face with a puzzled look to represent thinking and finally a matchstick figure of Jack sitting down relaxed against a tree. The staff discussed with Jack whether his outbursts were getting him what he wanted and he agreed that they were just getting him into trouble; he tearfully acknowledged that he might not be able to attend the day centre any more. Stop-think-relax was presented as a possibly better way of Jack achieving his goals. First of all, a member of staff modelled being Jack by getting angry that no cup of tea was available, only coffee, and Jack agreed that he 'shouldn't carry on like that'. Then Jack was handed the paper with the drawings and the scenario was again role-played with the member of staff verbalising the procedure thus:

> I must *stop* myself exploding just because they have got no tea and *think*, plug my brain in and switch on, I can have tea at home later, no one is being horrible, I will *relax* by squeezing and releasing this ball for a while.

Then Jack was invited to role-play the scene and praised for his performance. A member of staff then role-played another typical scene in which Jack was getting angry over someone using his crayons. Unfortunately, this led Jack to make some uncomplimentary remarks about another service user, Billy, whom he judged would be the most likely miscreant in such circumstances. This illustrates the difficulty that people with learning difficulties have in generalising learning. Rather than ignore Jack's comment as irrelevant to what was being taught, the staff member role-played the scene again but integrating his concerns to make it more tangible:

> I really wanted to do some crayoning now, it's not fair they are not here, it will be Billy who has taken them, I must *stop* exploding at him, plug my brain in and switch on, to *think* Billy is nice most of the time, he just forgets a bit, I will just *relax* as I walk over to him by taking a deep breath and breathing out slowly saying 'relax'.

Jack was then asked to role-play the scene and given feedback on his performance. The staff at the centre agreed to remind Jack of his piece of paper (which he kept folded in his pocket) whenever he became angry or there were potential flash-points. His mother was also informed of the strategy and she and his sister were encouraged to use 'stop-think-relax' with him at home.

Jack's mother also used the 'stop-think-relax' strategy to help Jack overcome his fear of crossing roads alone. First, she accompanied him verbalising

> It's going to happen again, I am going to be lying in the road, *stop* and *think*, other people are crossing this road so it must be OK for me if I look just once each way as I cross, all I have to do is *relax*, just breathe in deeply and out slowly.

Then she got Jack to do this while she stood waiting for him to cross a minor road and gradually progressing to more major roads. She explained to him that it was like doing dares in the swimming pool that had enabled him to swim. Jack returned to his swimming classes as his anxiety and anger decreased.

Mood over mood

The thrust of this chapter has been on managing your mood by getting you to have second thoughts about what you are saying to yourself and to invest in various behaviours. It is also possible to manage mood by replacing an emotion with another emotion.

Patrick had decided that a good way of minimising conflict with his teenage daughter was to keep out of her way for the first hour after she had come home from school. He then felt that this could not go on forever. He was fearful that at her first transgression (which were many on returning home) he would go ballistic and she would in return retaliate. At the time of these escalating conflicts he felt he could watch himself losing the plot and actually tell himself 'Don't do this', but to no avail. It was as if there were two Patricks, with Patrick One urging caution and the other, Patrick Two, who was as immature as his daughter. What he had noticed he had lost since his fall was his sense of humour. He decided to use his humour to talk Patrick Two around rather in the way he had been adept at talking around the drunken Paul, when the latter was in danger of making a nuisance of himself in a pub. At his next after-school conflict with his daughter, Patrick One asked Patrick Two, 'Have you lost your teddy?'

Angela was abused in childhood both physically and sexually by her parents. In her therapeutic writing of letters to them (that she did not post) she noted the absence of anger. She found this curious given their unspeakable behaviour. Angela reflected that she had constructed herself to be the very opposite of her parents but this meant that she had also forgone anger and that her total taboo on this emotion was inappropriate. She decided that when she felt vulnerable or had intrusive disturbing fantasies of her mother coming into her home and taking her daughters away from her, she would angrily defend the 11-year-old Angela, together with her daughters at the same age, then imagine physically overpowering her mother. Historically Angela's fantasies left her feeling depressed but they ceased to exert powerful negative effects once she legitimised anger as an appropriate response. She was in effect using one form of mood or imagery to control another form of mood or imagery.

Focusing anger on the right target

The development of uncharacteristic irritability is one of the diagnostic symptoms of post-traumatic stress disorder and is often expressed in inappropriate situations, e.g. road rage after a road traffic accident. Understandably this can lead to guilt feelings, in reaction to which the person can create a taboo on the emotion of anger. However, one of the functions of anger is to flag up when an injustice has been committed, without utilising the emotion of anger we may simply blame ourselves for every calamity.

Peter attended the inquest on the colleague who had fallen from scaffolding and was surprised at the obvious discomfort of the deceased's co-worker when he was questioned about whether they had jointly ignored safety procedures. For the first time, Peter began to experience some annoyance with the deceased but then excused his behaviour with 'Well, they were only young' and reverted to musing that he should have done more. Later he recounted his experiences at the inquest to his wife. She was outraged that he was not angry at the two young men and instead got angry with himself and everybody else. He realised that he really ought to focus the anger on where it properly belonged.

9

Managing sleep and pain

For some trauma victims there is little respite from the horrors of their experience. When they sleep the nightmares flood in and they become fearful of going to sleep, and to make the hell worse, pain may disturb their sleep and act as a reminder of their trauma. It seems likely that the neuro-circuitry of pain and emotion overlap and one affects the other. For example if you have a bit of a headache and you get a telephone call that you have just won the National Lottery, suddenly the headache is barely noticeable. Alternatively if you have just had a bad argument with your partner, the headache feels worse. The management of mood becomes doubly important for those whose post-traumatic stress symptoms are complicated by chronic pain, as negative mood will likely intensify the experience of pain.

Ian dreaded going to bed, knowing that it would take him hours to get to sleep; his mind would race from one worry to another but always come back to the shooting at the club. He had tried to deal with it by going to bed later and later but eighteen months after the shooting, it had reached the point of absurdity often not going to bed until 3 a.m. and his sleep was still broken. Very reluctantly he went to see his GP for help with the sleep and she prescribed the sleeping tablet, Zopiclone (7.5mg). This helped but it was still taking him an hour to get to sleep. He decided to put himself in a better frame of mind for sleep by listening to soft music on headphones for forty-five minutes before bedtime. Ian had noticed that sleep happened only when he was not trying to sleep, often nodding off briefly watching TV about 9 p.m. But in bed he was trying to force sleep and getting irritated with himself for not being asleep, which in turn made sleep more difficult. Ian decided to cut his losses: if he was not asleep within thirty minutes he would calmly get up and go back to bed only when he was really tired. His new sleep strategies helped but he was still getting about two hours less sleep a night than he was before the shooting – a time when he was exercising regularly. Since the shooting he hadn't exercised, partly because of his physical injuries but also partly because he was worried that in a gym he might meet someone associated with his previous work as a doorman and he did not want to run the remotest chance of a connection to the gunmen. So Ian decided to do what exercises he could with a multi-gym at home. He found that the daily exercise helped his sleep slightly and his mood. However, he was still troubled by the pain in his leg which in turn affected his sleep. Ian used the MOOD framework in Table 9.1 to identify and modify his thinking about his pain.

It is useful to monitor the intensity of pain using the scale in Table 9.2.

When Ian monitored his pain, his initial reaction was to think of it as awful but on reflection 'awful' would have been the worst pain he ever felt, which was when he was in hospital after the shooting and this merited a score of 8; his present discomfort was actually a 6. Thinking objectively about his pain, he guessed that it would become a more manageable 4 within the hour. He also thought he could make a slight difference by rubbing the affected area.

Tessa became preoccupied with whether she should have on amputation of her lower left leg. Her orthopaedic surgeons could give no guarantee that such an operation would relieve her pain, which they said may well simply move up her leg. She protested to her friend, Jane, that she did not know what to do and Jane retorted, 'Who does? So how can you?' Tessa realised that her quest for certainty was a pipe dream and that she was probably making her pain seem worse by the endless agonising. Further her sleep had become more fragmented since discussing with the surgeons the possibility of amputation. Jane

Table 9.1 **Ian's MOOD framework**

Monitor mood	**O**bserve thinking	**O**bjective thinking	**D**ecide what to do and do it
Mood dipped in the night when woken by the pain in my leg.	It's hopeless, nothing I can do about it, awful. I can't stand it.	I can make it a little easier by rubbing the area. It's not that awful, it's 6/8 using the Present Pain Intensity Scale. It will probably take an hour to subside to a manageable 4/8. I will be aware of the pain but I am not going to fuss over it.	If I am not asleep in half an hour I will just get up and let sleep and pain take care of themselves.

Table 9.2 **Present Pain Intensity Scale**

Very severe pain	8	Very severely disturbing/disabling
	7	
Severe pain	6	Markedly disturbing/disabling
	5	
Moderate pain	4	Definitely disturbing/disabling
	3	
Mild pain	2	Slightly disturbing/not really disabling
	1	
No pain	0	

suggested that they might try going swimming as a way of distracting her from 'picking' at the issue. But Tessa insisted that she needed to be certain that there would be no children in the pool and that she would not be too drained. Jane reminded her that before the riding accident she was full of life, took chances and now had to decide, 'Do you want to have a life or to be certain?' Tessa realised that she had to make commitments in the various domains of her life one way or the other and that it was probably more important to decide than what to decide.

Rumination

Ruminating or stewing over the frustration of not now being able to perform a particular task has more of an effect on your mood than the frustration itself.

In her riding accident Tessa had damaged not only her leg but also her right hand and she had had three operations on it. The surgeon was reluctant to do a fourth operation to increase the mobility of her small finger, explaining that repairing a repair was not usually a good idea. He advised extensive physiotherapy and Tessa duly attended sessions. While the physiotherapist was very nice, Tessa would leave the sessions feeling very angry. Her mood would be low for hours and she would be snappy. However, she was able to stop her ruminating after sessions using the MOOD framework in Table 9.3.

Unhelpful thinking about pain

Just as avoidance of feared situations can be overcome by daring oneself to gradually approach them, so the boundaries that pains impose can be explored by gradually daring oneself to encounter situations where pain may be anticipated. However, performing these behavioural experiments can be sabotaged by unhelpful thinking. The saboteurs can be immobilised by identifying and modifying the information processing biases. In Chapter 8 some of the biases in information processing that can serve to lower mood were introduced (Table 8.3) and there are a very similar set of biases

Table 9.3 **Tessa's MOOD framework**

Monitor mood	**O**bserve thinking	**O**bjective thinking	**D**ecide what to do and do it
Mood dips after physio, in more pain.	I cannot bend my little finger. I do the exercises at home but it's no use. She must think I am not doing them and I am not trying.	How do I know what she is thinking? I am not a mind-reader, maybe I should just ask her? Does it really matter anyway what she thinks? She will not lose sleep over it.	I will ask the physio what she thinks next time. For now I am going to visit my friend and not dwell on the pain.

that can result in an enhanced perception of pain and an exaggeration of the limitations it imposes.

The intensity of pain experienced is only partly related to the amount of tissue damage; it is also in part affected by the way in which the individual thinks about their pain. It has been found that those who catastrophise about their pain then experience it more intensely. There are three aspects to *catastrophisation*: magnification – exaggerating the degree of pain (e.g. Ian in Table 9.1), rumination – dwelling on the pain and its impact, and helplessness – believing that you cannot influence the pain (e.g. Ian in Table 9.1). If your mood dips in response to pain, it is useful to try to stand back and question whether you are magnifying the extent of the pain, minimising what you can do about it or perhaps dwelling on it.

There are a number of other information processing biases that can lead to a heightened sense of pain and of its restrictions (Table 9.4).

Table 9.4 **More biases in information processing**

1 *Lack of generalisation of corrective experience*: a discovery that though you may perform a particular action without due discomfort, e.g. lift the baby into her pram, you do not go on to perform equivalent actions, e.g. lift a similar weight to the same height.
2 *Over-generalisation of negative experience*: assuming that because pain was experienced in one particular context (e.g. shopping), pain is inevitable in the same context (e.g. shopping).
3 *Selective abstraction*: you experience some difficulty in one aspect of your life, e.g. not passing an exam, and you take it out of context, e.g. 'I am never going to qualify because of this back problem'.
4 *Jumping to conclusions*: the person experiences some difficulty but exaggerates the significance, e.g. 'I had some pain today swimming, pretty soon I won't be able to swim at all'.

The information processing biases can be monitored and corrected using the MOOD framework in Table 9.1.

While resignation to pain is unhelpful and reflects helplessness, an acceptance of pain has been found to be important to the management of pain. In order to focus on goals and the values they reflect, e.g. to be mobile enough to go on a night out with friends, there is an acceptance of some pain borne out of an overriding commitment to the maintaining of friendship (a value). The removal of the cognitive roadblocks to the exploration of the boundaries of your pain is a necessary precursor to achieving the type of life that you can value.

Monitoring pain

Many pain sufferers are reluctant to monitor their pain because they fear attending to it will make it worse. However, it is only necessary to spend at most thirty seconds, to record the intensity of pain using the Present Pain Intensity Scale (Table 9.2) and what you have been doing, these snapshots are repeated morning, afternoon and evening to create a pain diary. When pain is really bad, the temptation is to think that your pain is always bad, but the diary then acts as a reminder that this is not always the case. A section of Ian's diary is shown in Table 9.5.

Inspection of Ian's pain diary revealed that on Thursday morning he had managed his pain well: he and his wife had agreed beforehand that after their main shop in a supermarket they would sit and have a long coffee break and do a crossword in the newspaper before doing the rest of their shopping. He had agreed that in the afternoon he would be at his brother-in-law's new home to take delivery of items. As the afternoon moved on, he began to experience more pain in his leg but was too embarrassed to tell his brother-in-law he needed long breaks. Ian could see that his brother-in-law clearly needed a lot of help and he pushed himself to continue helping into the evening, even though the pain was worsening. The next morning he was in agony and unable to bear weight, with a slight improvement by Friday afternoon when he was able to collect his children from school. By evening he was demoralised and felt he had had a wasted day and blamed his brother-in-law,

Table 9.5 Ian's diary

Thursday	Action	Pain (0–8)
Morning	Went shopping with wife	3
Afternoon	Helped brother-in-law move house	5
Evening	Shifted furniture around at brother-in-law's	6

Friday	Action	Pain (0–8)
Morning	Didn't do anything, stayed in	8
Afternoon	Collected kids from school	7
Evening	Didn't do anything, couldn't be bothered returning phone call to brother-in-law	7

refusing to return his call. When challenged by his wife about not returning the call, he became angry and she remonstrated with him about whether her brother was supposed to be a mind-reader and admonished him to stop trying to prove himself physically: 'All any of us can do is make the best of what we have got'. Ian sulked after this but reluctantly acknowledged that there was much truth in what she said. He realised that he had to stop 'blitzing' things because he then paid for it with total inactivity and demoralisation. Ian resolved to keep to a steady pace of activity that he could keep to each day and that, as with his wife, he needed to 'go public' about his limitations. But then he had a thought that others would think less of him. Using the framework of Table 9.1, Ian came up with the more objective thought that he did not think less of others with physical limitations so why should they be thinking less of him. He mused, 'Maybe I've just become prejudiced against myself'.

Goals and pacing

An important part of finding yourself again after a trauma is the reinstitution of goals that reflect what is important to you. Physical injuries may mean that the goals cannot be identical to what was pursued before the trauma but distilling goals that are manageable and meaningful is essential. The experience of extreme trauma does prompt a re-examination of what is important. In deciding on goals I am reminded of a Jesuit hymn which includes the line 'What would you wish you had done when you are dying?' Committing to and focusing on goals or values makes it easier to tolerate or accept pain in pursuit of those objectives; this is the basis of Acceptance and Commitment Therapy (Hayes et al. 1999), a variant of cognitive behavioural therapy.

Ian was committed to being helpful to others and wished to continue to be so after the shooting, but the practical expression of the value needed some modification. In particular he needed to pace himself.

Pacing can be likened to driving a car at a steady 56 mph because it makes best use of the petrol in the tank, as opposed to the short-term gain of driving at 70 mph but resulting in the cutting out of the engine. Thus Ian would be most pursuing his values by committing to pacing himself.

Patrick's stock response to anyone in the aftermath of his fall when invited to do something was, 'I'll see how I am first' and he would live in waiting for the occasional 'good day'. Adopting a policy of making hay while the sun shines, on good days he would blitz whatever tasks needed to be done. This would then render him physically incapable for days and very morose. At the suggestion of his GP he attended a local pain management course run by physiotherapists and psychologists, who stressed the importance of his pacing himself. Patrick realised that by adopting pacing, what he could do on each day was now predictable and he could control it; he no longer had to ride the emotional roller coaster of good and bad days. He had attended a hydrotherapy pool as part of his physiotherapy after his fall and was delighted at the sense of freedom being in water gave him. He resolved to go swimming daily after his physiotherapy was complete. At his local pool he enjoyed the banter with the other swimmers; although it did not totally replace the camaraderie he had at work, he felt it was something. The exercise itself also helped to lift his mood.

Imagery and pain

Images have the power to capture attention and as such they are a potential distraction from ruminating on pain. The most effective images appear to be the ones that are tailored to the particular pain. The potency of the image arises largely from the emotion associated with it and the interweaving of a sensory dimension.

Patrick saw balloons very positively, associating them with his grandchild. At his pain management course he learnt to imagine a series of different colour balloons on his head and visualised a particular colour balloon being inflated by the pain and then being released and floating away into a blue sky, watching it, then a different colour balloon being inflated and released.

Ian noticed that as the pain in his leg became intense, it would become warm. He imagined an ice sculpture of his leg and 'watched' as the area of his leg that had become warmest very slowly melted the corresponding area of the sculpture. He felt that were he to touch the melting area, he could feel the 'coldness'. Ian continued to 'stare' at the melting sculpture. He found that the strategy worked best when his pain was moderate rather than severe.

Self Instruction Training for pain and sleep

Both pain and sleep problems are stressful events that can be coped with using Meichenbaum's (1985) Self Instruction Training (SIT) that was introduced in Chapter 8. SIT involves the use of coping self-statements as shown in Table 9.6.

Karen had had some problems with sleep ever since she could remember, but they became more pronounced after she was raped. She decided to prepare for going to bed by telling herself, 'All I have to do is to concentrate on listening to soft music on headphones' (Table 9.6 category 1). Inevitably, memories of the rape would come to mind and she would have to tell herself 'to just focus on the music' (Table 9.6 category 2). But she

Table 9.6 **Self Instruction Training examples**

1 *Preparing for the stressor*: e.g. 'I know there will be some pain going out with friends for the evening (acceptance) but I am pretty sure I can keep it manageable (antidote to helplessness)'.
2 *Encountering the stressor*: e.g. 'The pain is getting difficult, there's nowhere to sit in the pub, I did not anticipate this. I will just mention to my friends that we might need to move on to another pub or club and see if there is a seat over the next thirty minutes'.
3 *Coping with feeling overwhelmed*: e.g. 'It is getting busier, the pain is getting pretty bad. I'll just go the toilet, sit there a few minutes and then tell my friends we should move on'.
4 *Review of coping efforts/stressor*: e.g. 'The night out was OK. So long as I am clear with others about what I can and cannot do they are OK. What would be my next "dare"?'

would begin to feel overwhelmed when memories of the sexual abuse in childhood also intruded. She would tell herself, 'The memories are just the crackling of an old radio, I'll tap with alternate hands to the music and let the memories fade of their own accord' (Table 9.6 category 3 – this strategy is also a hybrid of detached mindfulness with regard to traumatic material and an EMDR-like technique). In reviewing the efficacy of the strategy, Karen decided to tell herself, 'At least I am doing something that should eventually help with sleep but I am also teaching myself the fear these memories bring is not a fear that I am afraid of'.

Sleep diary

Sleep disturbance often persists long after a trauma. Not only may the victim have difficulty getting off to sleep but also their sleep may often be broken by nightmares and/or pain. To cope with these difficulties, many take increasing amounts of alcohol. While this may help the individual get off to sleep, the brain does not go through the same cycles as in natural sleep. As a result, although the person may have been rendered unconscious, it is not a refreshing, energising sleep; indeed it is a sleep not worth having. Further alcohol is a depressant, serving to lower mood next morning, making its management that much more difficult. Low mood following trauma means that you may in fact be getting more sleep than you imagine, albeit that it is less than you want. By completing a sleep diary (see Table 9.7) you can get an accurate picture of your sleep pattern and importantly identify what makes it better and worse.

Ian's battle with sleep began even before he went to bed. He became agitated that he would be restless for hours, disturbing his wife, and he was terrified of having a nightmare of the shooting. He tried to cope by going later and later to bed but then did not want to take his child to school. Ian forced himself to take his son to school but went back to bed afterwards. He then felt he had wasted the morning and became low and irritable. At his wife's suggestion they decided to go shopping after taking their son to school.

Table 9.7 **Sleep diary**

Week:	Time to get off to sleep, after putting head on pillow	Duration of sleep episodes	Total sleep	Strategies
Sunday				
Monday				
Tuesday				
Wednesday				
Thursday				
Friday				
Saturday				

As a rough rule of thumb, for every ten minutes slept in the day, twenty minutes are lost in the night. It is often a struggle to begin with to alter the body clock so that daytime sleeping is avoided. While there are unhelpful coping strategies such as daytime sleeping and alcohol abuse, there are also helpful strategies, both of which can be detailed in column five of Table 9.7. When Ian completed his diary, he was surprised to find that he was in fact getting on average five hours' sleep a night. He was not too impressed when his wife told him that Mrs Thatcher, the former prime minister, managed on five hours a night but took the point. Ian recognised that his desire for eight hours' sleep a night was inappropriate, given how little energy he now expended each day. His wife pointed out that it was his irritability over his sleep in bed that disturbed her much more than his restlessness. Ian noted that he became irritable if he wasn't asleep within thirty minutes and decided to calmly get up if not asleep within twenty or thirty minutes, returning to bed only when really tired. In this way his bed would become associated with sleep rather than a battle. He reasoned that sleep tended to happen when he was not trying.

Rescripting nightmares

Nightmares of an extreme trauma are commonplace and usually gradually reduce in frequency over the first twelve months, but despite this may still occur several times a week. The nightmares usually break the person's sleep or result in a very restless sleep. The next day the person is likely to dwell on the nightmare resulting in a lowering of mood and an associated irritability, which in turn strains relationships.

The nightmares are often variations of what happened in the actual trauma but involving a worse outcome. Alternatively the nightmare may end at the worst point in the trauma, catapulting the individual into distressed wakefulness and disorientation. Whatever form the nightmare takes, it does not reflect the whole story of the trauma and it probably reflects an incomplete processing of the trauma in the day. One view of dreams is that they represent the unfinished business of the day, but another view is that they are the rubbish bin of the mind. The truth of the matter is probably somewhere between the two extreme views.

There is some evidence that deliberately calling to mind your typical nightmare in the early evening, and imagining its transformation, gradually results in the integration of the latter into it, resulting in less disturbance.

Ian's nightmare always finished as he was looking down the barrel of the gun, thinking 'This is it'. He realised that this was an incomplete picture of his experience in that he survived, and therefore decided to transform the image by visualising the gun discharging a banner of his favourite football team. At about 8 p.m. each evening he practised for a few minutes imaging this antidote. It took him two weeks before the new image was integrated into his dreams and he became less fearful of sleep.

John's nightmares were worse than what actually happened to him in that he had the severe burns that his colleague Alan had suffered in the gas explosion. During the day he daydreamed about what it would have been like to have been as physically injured as Alan was, and considered himself 'weird' for such thoughts. In the early evening John called to mind the vision of himself in his nightmares, then visualised himself unzipping a wet suit and taking off the suit gradually to reveal himself as he was now: 'Not a pretty sight in any case', he mused. Like Ian, it took him a couple of weeks before the new image replaced the old in his dreams and his sleep was less disturbed.

Cecilia's nightmares were usually a bizarre twist to what happened in that her car would stop and she, Amanda, Abigail and Anthony were emptied out of the rear from a great height and she would wake at this point distressed. She decided to capitalise on the 'ridiculousness' of the dream by imagining in the early evening that they all fell from the car onto a bouncy castle that Abigail continued to play on and she then assists her off the castle. It took Cecilia a couple of weeks before the transformation was grafted into her nightmares and she become less fearful of them.

10

Old baggage, new trauma

You may be more vulnerable than most to the effects of an extreme trauma in that you may carry the scars of other battles. It may be that you had previously suffered from a psychological disorder, recovered, only to succumb again in the wake of the trauma resulting in the coexistence of two or more disorders (co-morbidity).

Sam had abused alcohol twenty years before his accident: he had worked on a building site where it was very much the custom, after a hard day's work, to go to the pub. He attended Alcoholics Anonymous and had largely abstained from alcohol until his road traffic accident. Following the accident, he found sleep very difficult and within three months was again abusing alcohol. However, a legacy of the earlier alcohol abuse was that he had a low self-esteem. This had mattered little, because the praise of work colleagues for work well done and the support of his wife nullified his low self-esteem. But after the accident he was subjected to criticism both at home and in work. He could not stand what he saw as an onslaught on his self-esteem and alcohol became a way of drowning his sorrows.

It is useful to chart the influence of 'old baggage' by constructing a timeline depicting the view of self ('I am . . .'), view of personal world ('Life is . . .') and coping strategies ('So I . . .'). See Table 10.1 for Sam's timeline.

Reading Table 10.1 from left to right, the previous triad of 'I am . . .', 'Life is . . .', 'So I . . .' (first row) sets the scene for vulnerability to the effects of the next major life event (second row). The final triad of Table 10.1 (bottom line) makes it

Table 10.1 Sam's timeline

Major life events	Age	I am . . .	Life is . . .	So I . . .
Parents' divorce	8	Vulnerable	Uncertain	Try to please everyone
Working on building site, want to fit in, drink too much	21	Not up to much	Uncertain	Compensate by working extremely hard and being devoted to my family
Road traffic accident	40	Very vulnerable, I am a failure	Uncertain and dangerous	Become a control freak, comfort myself with alcohol, isolate myself

easier to understand why Sam was much more vulnerable to excessive self-blame over his children's involvement in the accident.

While a person might not have been previously diagnosed as having a psychiatric disorder, they may nevertheless have had to struggle to cope with abuse as a child or marginalisation compared to siblings. In response to their psychologically toxic childhood, they may have developed coping strategies that were effective at the time but are no longer viable post trauma, making recovery from their trauma more difficult.

Karen was sexually abused by her cousin as a child and raped by her partner as an adult. Her timeline is shown in Table 10.2.

Looking down the 'I am . . .' column in Table 10.2, Karen's self-dislike steadily increases until the time she is 18 and it has become a deep-rooted prejudice. In Karen's case she was attributing all of her 'stupidity' and feelings of being 'dirty' to the rape, but in looking at her timeline she was able to

Table 10.2 **Karen's timeline**

Major life events	*Age*	*I am . . .*	*Life is . . .*	*So I . . .*
Abuse by cousin	8–11	Damaged goods	Scary	Cling on to whoever seems strong
Abuse laxatives, cut myself	17	Unattractive, helpless	Uncertain	Take whatever relationships are on, take control of weight and of feeling something by cutting self
Raped by partner	18	I am stupid, dirty	A jungle	Isolate myself

construct a 'responsibility pie' for the factors involved in her prejudice against herself. Karen's pie is shown in Figure 10.1.

As Karen constructed the responsibility pie (working clockwise from her earliest years) she became aware that her parents,

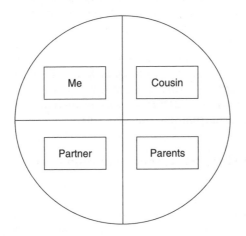

Figure 10.1 **Karen's responsibility pie.**

whom she loved, could have taken more time to try to find out why she had taken on overdose at age 11 and if they had, perhaps her negative self-image would not have taken root. She concluded that she should no more blame herself than her parents and that she, like them, was no more than 25 per cent responsible for the way she felt about herself. Further, she could still regard her parents as 'good' people and in theory at least could regard herself as 'good'.

Finding 'ME' again

If you have had a single extreme trauma as an adult it is relatively easy to find yourself again after a period of destabilisation (see Chapter 9). But if you have had previous traumas (like Karen in Table 10.2) the 'me' that you are try-ing to rediscover is likely to be unstable and negative reflect-ing the developmental age of the earlier traumas. The earlier memory will need to be superseded by an updated memory that recognises the emotions and bodily feelings of the early experience but introduces a compassionate adult perspec-tive. However, the earlier memory is not erased but can be circumvented by the competing 'new' memory.

In Karen's case she 'updated' the early memory by recalling the 11-year-old Karen and where she was and how she felt when she realised she had been 'stupid'. She then comforted her by telling her that there had never been a little Karen with an adult's knowledge and she was not 'stupid'. Karen cuddled a cushion to represent the younger self, so that she could feel the new knowledge – a corrective emotional experience. The effect of this was that she did not feel just as she had done before the rapes but better than she had ever felt.

Distinguishing background emotion from current emotion

The earlier traumatic experiences may create a background emotion that may be similar in nature to that generated by the later trauma and this makes it likely that all distress is attributed to the most recent event. Karen initially put all her distress down to the rape but after a few months realised that 80 per cent of her negative feelings about herself were attributable to the rape and the other 20 per cent predated the trauma. Emotional intelligence involves recognising what emotions are about in order to be able to manage them. It is not possible to comprehensively address current emotion without taking into account any distressing background emotion.

High levels of expressed emotion

High levels of criticism or over involvement have been found to be psychologically toxic: sufferers from depression and schizophrenia are more likely to relapse when exposed to high levels of *expressed emotion*. Similarly recovery from PTSD with cognitive behavioural therapy is detrimentally affected by high expressed emotion. It is possible to withstand high expressed emotion without developing a psychological disorder but in the wake of an extreme trauma, you may not have the emotional resources and your trauma response may be complicated by the development of depression as a coexisting disorder.

Joan had coped with her hypercritical husband before the mugging by maintaining a variety of interests and friends. However, as a consequence of her panic attacks she stayed at home more, exposing herself to the 'toxic fumes' from her husband and within six months of the mugging had developed depression. She felt trapped, her parents were aged so she did not want to trouble them, and she did not have the financial resources to get a place of her own. Further she did not want to disrupt her daughter's exams by moving school. Her daughter broke the entrapment by insisting that she was going to live with her maternal grandparents and reluctantly Joan sought the support of her parents, who were less critical of her than she had imagined. Joan's depression began to lift but she did wonder why she had not removed herself from the 'fumes' long before the mugging and mused that perhaps the mugger did her a favour after all.

11

Managing additional disorders

Post-traumatic stress disorder often occurs in association with another disorder and the co-morbid disorder will usually need a special focus. With PTSD an associated disorder is the rule rather than the exception. In this chapter special consideration is given to the additional complications of alcohol abuse or dependence, obsessive compulsive disorder, social phobia, depression, generalised anxiety disorder and panic disorder.

Alcohol abuse or dependence

If you are suffering from post-traumatic stress there is about a 50 per cent chance of succumbing to alcohol abuse or dependence. Often the increased use begins with taking more alcohol than usual to help get off to sleep or to cope with flashbacks, then steadily more alcohol is needed to achieve the same effect. You are really drinking too much when your drinking is interfering with close relationships, work, obligations to others or with the law.

Sam went to see his GP about his alcohol consumption after his road traffic accident and they agreed a withdrawal programme involving the use of tranquilisers over a three-week period. There had been only one period since the accident when Sam had not been drinking heavily: this had lasted a few days and he had experienced withdrawal symptoms, sweating, palpitations and nausea. Sam was so disconcerted by the withdrawal symptoms that he remained drinking to comfort himself. He decided this time to enlist the support of his GP, who told him that he was not just abusing alcohol but had become alcohol dependent. The GP also explained to him that coming off alcohol was actually the easy bit; it was staying off that was the really difficult part.

Sam decided that he would taper off his drinking over a two-week period by first not drinking at all until after 7 p.m. then gradually putting back the starting time. When tempted to drink, he reminded himself that what he was really committed to was his family and work but to make these commitments powerful enough to override his desire for drink, he needed to make them graphic and compelling. So Sam decided to imagine the joy and excitement of Christmas morning with his wife and children and for work he imagined a team-building day in which they went paint-balling. By way of contrast he also imagined two worst case scenarios of his continued drinking: saying goodbye to his children because his wife had thrown him out of their home and clearing his work desk by putting the contents into plastic bags because he had agreed to leave rather than be dismissed for smelling of drink.

Sam's imagery strategies worked very well and he had abstained from drink for about six weeks when he was watching a film on TV. Quite unexpectedly it featured a road traffic accident that was identical to his own. He left the room immediately. His wife tried to calm him by saying, 'It's just a film' but this only made him angrier and he replied, 'I know it's just a film, that's what makes my reaction so stupid'. His wife then became angry, and he stormed out of the house and went for a walk. After about thirty minutes he had calmed a little, passed a pub and thought, 'I'll just have a pint before going home'. After he had had one pint, he felt guilty and thought, 'Might as well be hung for a sheep as for a lamb!' By the time he got home, he was the worse for the drink and his wife was decidedly not amused. The ensuing fracas woke one of the children, who came downstairs visibly upset.

Sam was distraught by his relapse and booked an appointment to see his GP again. The latter reminded him of Mark Twain's dictum about smoking: 'Giving up smoking is easy, I have done it hundreds of times'. Sam explained the coping strategies he had been using and the GP said they were excellent strategies, but that he needed to see slips as opportunities to learn from mistakes. He said that Sam's first mistake was in not simply accepting his experience of intense emotion at an unexpected reminder of his road traffic accident and that he needed to cultivate an acceptance rather than berating himself. Further the slip suggested he was vulnerable to relapse when his mood dipped and there was conflict. He needed to remind himself that his coping strategies were particularly important to use then. Finally his GP pointed out that he needed to be aware of apparently irrelevant decisions such as 'I'll just have one pint' – that the relapses are often subtle seductions. Sam found it interesting when the GP explained that there is no biological reason why one drink should lead to another and that a slip does not have to become a full-blown relapse. Provided he did not overdo the guilt when he had a slip he could learn from it and see a further drink as a choice not a necessity. They agreed that realistically they ought to budget for gradually greater time gaps between slips and in this way he could still pursue the goals in life that were important to him.

Obsessive compulsive disorder

About one-third of those suffering from PTSD develop obsessive compulsive symptoms such as repeatedly checking that doors are locked or the gas is switched off, and excessive cleaning and tidying. The more time devoted to these 'safety' procedures, the greater the degree of impairment. If the checking goes on for hours the person would probably be regarded as having obsessive compulsive disorder (OCD) but you may engage in lesser levels of checking which nevertheless are a definite inconvenience and you would be regarded as having a sub-syndromal level of OCD.

Cecilia found that after her car accident, it was taking her about half an hour to get out of the house when she was by herself because she would repeatedly check that she had locked her front door and switched off household appliances; as a consequence she was often late for appointments. However, she did much less checking if she was with her husband or daughters. At first she thought she checked less when accompanied because of embarrassment but then she realised that it was actually because she felt the responsibility for 'safety' was somehow shared. (It seemed to echo not wanting full responsibility for passengers since the accident.) To her surprise she checked the security of her home less even when accompanied only by her 6-year-old daughter Abigail, which made little sense as the latter was objectively not going to enhance safety. Cecilia's key problem was an excessive sense of responsibility and a need to feel certain that she had made things safe.

Cecilia began to address her obsessive compulsive disorder by mentally putting strange labels on tasks that she was prone to repeat. When she was locking her front door she said 'red octopus', then when she was halfway down her road and tempted to return 'just once more' to see that she had done what she had planned to do, the strange phrase 'red octopus' would come to mind, reminding her that there was no need to check. Every couple of days she changed the strange label. She also realised that she was winding herself up with her quest for feelings of absolute certainty, that tolerating some uncertainty is an inevitable and necessary part of living.

Cecilia also found that following the accident she was spending her evenings cleaning. Much to the irritation of her family she would get up and clean, dust or wash in the middle of TV programmes. While she would have regarded herself as 'house-proud' before the accident, it had now reached an absurd level. She decided to gradually reduce her cleaning in the evening by not starting until after she had watched her favourite TV soap and permitting herself to interrupt this programme only at the adverts when she allowed herself to make a drink but not to clean. Her basic strategy was to gradually expose herself to the circumstance in which she would usually become obsessive and then prevent the obsessive response. After her first week of exposure and response prevention, she extended it by additionally not cleaning during the 10 o'clock News. Cecilia mused that she had felt out of control in the accident and that her cleaning was perhaps a bizarre way of proving to herself that at least she could control something, the cleanliness of her home.

Social phobia

About one in six sufferers with PTSD develop social phobia in which they feel they are the centre of others' attention
and are being negatively evaluated because of some perceived imperfection, e.g. blushing, stammering. As a consequence they begin to avoid situations in which they are in
the limelight.

After she was raped, Karen began to make excuses not to meet
up with friends: she was finding her encounters with them a
strain. It was as if when she was with them, she was standing
outside of herself criticising herself for not really having anything interesting to say and stammering when she did say
something. Further she saw herself as 'frumpy' compared to her
attractive friends. On one occasion she had arrived unexpectedly early to meet a friend at a café, sat with a coffee, became
conscious of her hand shaking slightly as she lifted her cup and
of the act of swallowing, and wondered whether others had
noticed. To her alarm she caught sight of a couple looking in
her direction and she left the café. Later Karen telephoned her
friend to apologise; the latter was irate telling her that she had
gone through two cups of coffee waiting for her. Karen tried to
explain her anxiety but her friend with characteristic sarcasm
replied, 'So everybody else has got nothing better to do than
sit around Karen and mark her out of ten as a human being
depending on whether her hand shakes or she gulps, what is
worse a gulp or a shake?' She was offended by her friend's tone
and put the phone down on her. When she had calmed down a
little, she realised that since the rapes she thought she was at
the centre of other people's universe. Karen reluctantly
acknowledged that she was probably no more being 'marked'
in the café than her friend was; indeed the only critic was
herself.

The sufferer from social phobia has acquired a story of
interaction with others that is very adolescent like. It is akin
to a 14-year-old male attributing his lack of success with girls
to his slight acne and endlessly agonising about his blem-
ishes. An adult talking to this 14-year-old boy would probably
try to make him aware of the complexities of relationships.

Recovery from social phobia requires an updating of the story of social interaction. This can be constructed by slow motion action replays of situations in which there has been social avoidance, such as of Karen in the café. Applying the MOOD framework of Chapter 9 to this situation, Karen's observed thinking might have been, 'They are looking at me, thinking I am an idiot, shaking and gulping my coffee'. While a more objective perspective might be, 'The couple are probably more interested in each other than me, anyone looking at their hand holding a cup long enough will probably make it shake more but who would be bothered'. The 'D' of the MOOD framework, 'Decide what to do and do it', may have been a decision not only to stay in the café and await her friend's arrival but also in future social contexts to remind herself that a critical spotlight is not on her.

As with other disorders, in social phobia not only is it the content of thinking that is exaggeratedly negative but also there are biases in information processing (see Table 8.3 on page 99).

After the rapes Karen used all or nothing thinking when judging other people's responses to her; either they were obviously very positive to her or they disapproved of her. She had lost any notion that people could be neutral about her. When Karen finally plucked up the courage to ring her friend and apologise for putting the phone down on her, after discussing her poor self-image, the friend suggested that she should look at the photograph of their school reunion and list them all in order of 'frumpiness' and only then locate herself. The friend said she would also do a 'frumpy list' and they would meet and compare notes. When they met the friend had placed Karen in the middle of the list and to Karen's surprise she had placed herself only a little lower. At the end of their meeting, Karen reluctantly agreed that she was 'not that bad', that some of the 'stick insects' were not very nice people and that some of the more 'frumpy' ones were really nice. After her friend had left, Karen pondered whether it mattered much at all where she was on her or her friend's list.

Depression

Depression and post-traumatic stress disorder have many overlapping symptoms such as impaired concentration and disturbed sleep and it is unsurprising that about half of those with PTSD also meet diagnostic criteria for depression. Nevertheless when there is an additional diagnosis of depression and the depression is regarded as moderate or severe, special attention needs to be directed at it.

John had post-traumatic stress disorder and severe depression following the gas explosion at work. While he managed to force himself back to work six months after the explosion, on his days off he would lie in bed most of the day; he would then be angry at himself for having wasted so much time. His lethargy was more a feature of his depression than his PTSD. But once he got down over his inactivity, he would brood about the explosion and its effects thereby maintaining his PTSD symptoms.

Recovery from depression involves two major components, the first is *activity scheduling* and the second is *mood management*. John realised that by taking to his bed on his days off, he was not investing in life and that if there were no investments, there could be no return. His mood, as is common with many people suffering from depression, was worse in the morning and on his days off he could not be bothered to get started. He decided that he could not afford the luxury of being governed by his mood and each evening, before his day off, he would make a timetable of the next day and approach it as if they were requirements of his workplace. In order to ensure that he got up in the morning, he placed his alarm on the other side of the room, which necessitated his having to get out of bed to switch it off. Although the timetable got him started on his days off, he quickly became frustrated because tasks such as 'sort out the garden' seemed too big. John decided that in order to make his timetable viable, the tasks he needed to set himself had to be small and specific with breaks between. He found that a timetable that read 'mow front lawn, have a cup of tea, mow front lawn, go for a walk to buy evening newspaper', worked out much better than bigger and vaguer tasks. John also addressed his mood using the MOOD framework, as we saw in Table 8.2 (page 97).

Depression can be a trauma response together with other disorders in which there is no significant symptom overlap.

Joan suffered from panic disorder with severe agoraphobic avoidance and depression after she was mugged. Just as smoking might cause different disorders such as heart disease and cancer in the same person, so an extreme trauma can cause different disorders. After she was mugged Joan became afraid to go out by herself and she missed out on many of the activities that used to lift her mood, such as going to town for shopping and visiting relatives. The panic disorder with severe agoraphobic avoidance set the scene for the development of depression. At home Joan could not be bothered with her cross-stitching or developing her family history on the internet. She decided to tackle her inactivity at home first, because activity at home seemed not to trigger panic attacks. Joan timetabled in fifteen-minute slots of cross-stitching or genealogy followed by a few minutes' break. Her concentration was sufficient for these brief periods and gradually she derived pleasure from her activities and had a sense of achievement at the end of the day. This in turn helped her sleep better.

Despite her increased activity level, Joan's mood was often unaccountably low. Her hypercritical husband became even angrier than usual at such times and protested on one occasion, 'If a car stops working, something has gone wrong!' Much as she was annoyed at being compared to a car, she realised that if she carefully tracked the downturns in her mood, she might discover what was upsetting and then work out what could be done about it. Joan adopted a 'stop, think, act' approach to every lowering of her mood. She was surprised to find that it was often her response to everyday minor hassles, e.g. mother-in-law dropping in, that got her down as opposed to the bigger problems of panic attacks and difficulties in going out alone. The monitoring of mood is the necessary first step (M) in using the MOOD framework from Chapter 8, and Joan's 'stop, think' embraces the observation of thinking (first O) and objective thinking (second O), while her 'act' is the equivalent of the D of MOOD, decide what to do and do it. Her 'stop, think, act' stopped her endlessly dwelling (depressive rumination) on the mugging.

A recurring theme for Joan was 'I am crap' and on one of her mother's visits, she broke down crying that she was a 'waste of space'. Her mother comforted her as she had done in childhood. Joan said that she felt a failure as a mother and wife, and with characteristic candour her mother said, 'What mother does not feel a failure at times. It would be a lot easier if your so-called husband just occasionally backed your decisions'.

The perceived non-performance of an important role often ushers in depression. Questioning whether the role performance should be viewed so negatively can lead to a lifting of mood (see Chapter 8).

Generalised anxiety disorder

About 40 per cent of those suffering from PTSD have an additional diagnosis of generalised anxiety disorder. The key feature of generalised anxiety disorder is uncontrollable worry about a wide range of matters.

Maureen had always regarded herself as a 'bit of a worrier' even before being thrown forward on the bus; indeed she had been this way ever since she could remember, but it was only afterwards that her worry became uncontrollable. Maureen and her friend attended a night school class on managing stress. Though it was an anxiety management group, the group was very large and discussion of personal problems was not permitted. At the end of the ten weekly sessions, she listed what for her had been the important things that she had learnt (see Table 11.1). Maureen was pleased to learn that though anxiety did express itself in her body with headaches and general tension, this did not lead to anything serious. Since her fall on the bus, she had been conscious that her uncle had died following a stroke and she had vague thoughts that all her strain might result in a similar fate. She had also found it very useful to write down her reflex automatic thoughts when she got upset and then to stand back from them and come up with a more rational response using the MOOD

Table 11.1 **Maureen's key ideas**

---

1 Worry does no physical harm.
2 I need to challenge positive beliefs about worry, e.g. my worry stops return of daughter's cancer.
3 I need to challenge negative beliefs about worry, e.g. it will cause a heart attack.
4 To help do 2 and 3 I can use MOOD (see Chapter 8).
5 Some of my beliefs are unhelpful, e.g. worrying proves I care, actions speak louder.
6 The best way of dealing with worry is to postpone it to a worry half-hour.
7 I am better off accepting that there is always some uncertainty.
8 I can relax using a relaxation exercise or using my exercise bike.

---

record (Chapter 8). To her surprise in completing her Thought Record (MOOD) she found she had some strange positive beliefs about worry as if it was somehow magical and deserving of praise. Maureen found that when she postponed her worries to a fixed half-hour (on the basis that half-an-hour's worry a day is more than enough for anyone) to be worked out properly on paper, the worry she had had usually evaporated by her chosen time. She also realised that she exhausted herself by trying to be certain of everything. Maureen had nearly not attended the night school class because her friend could not provide enough reassurance about who they would meet there. Maureen was particularly struck by the idea of testing out negative predictions rather then assuming they are automatically true. She reflected that her prediction that everyone there would be weird was not borne out. She enjoyed chatting to people at the coffee break and was relieved that she did not have to take a seat near the exit because of panic attacks, like a pleasant and not at all 'weird' lady she met called Emma. Maureen bought a relaxation tape: the exercises on it involved the alternate tensing and relaxing of muscles and she found this helpful. On the course they were advised to exercise three times a week and to her surprise she found that after a twenty-minute session on her exercise bike, problems that she was worrying about before did not seem as big.

Panic disorder

About one in four of those who suffer PTSD develop panic disorder, although the latter does not necessarily develop immediately after the trauma. In Chapter 2 it was explained that the brain's alarm (the amygdala) is involved in both PTSD and panic disorder. The hypersensitive alarm that develops in PTSD responds to external reminders, while in panic disorder the 'dodgy alarm' is triggered by unusual but not necessarily abnormal bodily sensations. If the initial panic symptoms are seen as a catastrophe, e.g. 'My heart is racing, this means I am going to have a heart attack', the panic symptoms increase further. In turn they may be catastrophically misinterpreted, e.g. 'It's getting worse, I am going to die' and a vicious circle is set up leading to a full-blown panic attack.

Emma developed many post-traumatic stress symptoms after she tripped getting out of a taxi while pregnant. These symptoms cleared up soon after the uneventful birth of her child, only to be replaced a few weeks later by panic attacks and a fear of going out alone outside her neighbourhood. Emma decided to attend a night school stress management class and met Maureen there. At a coffee break she told her that since the previous week's class she had had a bad panic attack at the checkout at their local supermarket and abandoned her shopping. Emma said that she felt better when she got outside; she went home but then felt an 'idiot'. The class that night had been on behavioural experiments (testing out whether your negative predictions are true) and Emma told Maureen that she was going to see if anything really bad would happen if she stayed in the supermarket while having a panic attack. However, Maureen noticed that as Emma was telling her about her last panic attack, she became agitated. Maureen asked her if she was OK. Emma replied, 'This is stupid – just talking about it is getting my heart racing. I am starting to sweat, I feel faint, I don't want to make a show of myself here, I will have to go'. Maureen suggested, 'Here is a very good place to start with a behavioural experiment. See if anything terrible does happen if you do not leave the class'. Emma answered, 'OK I'll just sit down'. Maureen protested, 'No, no, you can't learn that you would not faint anyway if you sit down'. So for the rest of the coffee break, Emma continued to stand and she focused on the sort of week that Maureen had had since the last class. By the time they were asked by the group leader to resume their places, Emma noticed that most of her panic symptoms had gone and she had learnt that she did not in fact faint if she did not sit down. As she took her place, she mused that if she could bring on her panic symptoms just by talking about them, they cannot be that serious as it is not possible to bring on a heart attack or a stroke just by talking about them.

Emma had learnt in her night school class that it is extremely unusual to faint during a panic attack, because in most attacks the heart races, which means blood pressure is going up, while fainting requires a lowering of blood pressure. Although she found this interesting information, it was knowledge with her head (what is technically termed declarative knowledge) and not knowledge with her guts (procedural knowledge). It was not until she dared herself not to sit down when having a panic attack with Maureen that she really understood that she would not faint. Away from the situation, sufferers from panic attacks often know they pose no real threat, but this knowledge seems to escape them when confronted with the onset of symptoms. It is therefore necessary for the sufferer to also learn in the actual situation that there is no threat. Emma decided to confront the supermarket once more and agreed to visit Maureen afterwards as she lived nearby.

Emma found that she was once again panicky in the supermarket and particularly so as she approached the queue at the checkout. This time she had decided just to let her feelings 'ride the Big Dipper', symptoms building up then reducing, in the knowledge that the worst would pass in five or ten minutes and she could report her success to Maureen. At one point Emma again wanted to run out of the shop, but she likened this to being near the top of the 'Big Dipper': getting off now was not a good idea, but if she hung on a little longer she would be over the top and coming down the other side. She arrived at Maureen's home having successfully navigated the checkout and they celebrated over a cup of coffee. Maureen noticed but did not comment on Emma holding a bottle of water in her hand throughout the visit. The next week Emma again visited Maureen after shopping and was pleased to report that her panic symptoms at the checkout had been much less intense and she had not wanted to escape. Once again they celebrated with a coffee and Maureen could not help quizzing her, 'Is that the same bottle of water?' Emma laughed embarrassed and replied, 'Probably is'. To which Maureen queried, 'Is it a safety thing, like you used to sit down if you were having a panic attack?' Emma said, 'It has probably been my dummy since I tripped getting out of the taxi when pregnant! Here's me trying to get the baby off a dummy and I've got one myself: I must wean myself off it'.

Gradually letting go of safety procedures, e.g. going out only accompanied, is an important part of tackling panic disorder (see Chapter 5 to read Joan's 'Big Dipper' strategies).

12

Children and adolescents

Unfortunately children and adolescents are not exempt from the slings and arrows of outrageous fortune. It is tempting for adults to minimise the distress of children, to acknowledge it means running the risk of feeling their pain and experiencing a sense of helplessness and powerlessness. Studies of children involved in natural disasters have shown that parents and teachers under-report symptoms of post-traumatic stress and that when children have been asked directly about any difficulties, a different picture tends to emerge. In part the non-identification of symptoms in children and adolescents may arise because the child does not wish to upset the adult. This may particularly be the case if the adult has been distressed by the same trauma.

The way in which a traumatic stress reaction is expressed varies with the age of the child. Cecilia's three children, Anthony (aged 3), Abigail (aged 6) and Amanda (aged 14) each reacted differently to the road traffic accident they were in. Each of the children had therefore to be helped in different ways.

The pre-school child

Children under 4 years of age do not have the language abilities to be able to volunteer some of the symptoms of post-traumatic stress disorder such as feelings of detachment or estrangement from others, restricted range of affect (e.g. unable to have loving feelings) and sense of a foreshortened future. With regard to those symptoms that are private events, it is difficult for an adult to know what the toddler is feeling. It is not surprising therefore that when Scheeringa et al. (2003) studied a group of toddlers who had been traumatised, they found that no child met the DSM-IV criteria for PTSD, but when they used criteria that focused more on the child's behaviour and took account of their previous usual behaviour, 26 per cent met the criteria. As it is the case that a significant minority of adults suffer PTSD following an extreme trauma, it is to be expected that a similar proportion of trauma-exposed toddlers would share the same fate, making Scheeringa's criteria probably more applicable.

Both the DSM-IV and Scheeringa's criteria acknowledge that toddlers sometimes play out their trauma in a game and this can be taken as evidence that they are re-experiencing the trauma. Pre-school children may also re-experience their trauma in a variety of other ways such as nightmares, flashbacks or distress at exposure to reminders of the event. Scheeringa's criteria highlight the importance of assessing whether after the trauma the child has gone back to doing things he/she did when they were younger or has become more socially withdrawn. Scheeringa's criteria also focus on whether the toddler has developed new fears, such as separation anxiety, fear of toileting alone or fear of the dark and whether there is increased aggression.

Cecilia was concerned that after their road traffic accident, her 3-year-old son, Anthony, began bed-wetting; she was very frustrated at this because he had been out of nappies a year earlier. It was also much more difficult to leave him at nursery: she found it distressing that the staff had to 'peel him off' her, on the two days a week she left him there. At home she was disturbed to see that he played crashing his cars; matters were compounded further when he insisted on going to sleep with one of his parents present and was being aggressive, biting other children. Since the accident Anthony was waking in the night in a state of terror but unable to say what was awakening him and insisting that one of his parents was present until he returned to sleep. Although frustrated at the changes in Anthony after the accident, Cecilia had thought they would be short-lived, but when there were still problems four months after the accident, she sought the advice of her health visitor. The health visitor suggested that when she saw Anthony crash the cars, she should join in the game by having one of the car with people in and then taking out one of the occupants, soothing them by cuddling them and saying, 'Better now' and then getting the 'person' to say, 'Kick a ball'. The idea was that Anthony would thereby create and respond to an updated memory of the incident in which all is well, rather than the original version. When Cecilia did this, Anthony soon copied her lead. The health visitor suggested that she might benefit from attending a Group Parent Training Programme not only in relation to Anthony's difficulties but also with regard to 6-year-old Abigail's disruptive behaviour since the accident.

School-age children

The older the child, the more apt is the language of post-traumatic stress disorder as a description of the child or adolescent's difficulties. But even in adolescence, there may be a reversion to behaviours that have long since been out-grown, such as thumb-sucking. Further in the wake of a trauma the school-age child may show new symptoms of anxiety such as nail-biting or about being separated from parents. The increased anxiety is often accompanied by an increase in disobedience that may extend beyond home to school, interfering with studies. It is also possible for the school-age child to suffer from much the same range of additional disorders (e.g. panic disorder, obsessive compulsive disorder) that the adult might suffer from. The strategies that have been described so far in this book for adults have to be adapted to match the age of the child.

Abigail was still having nightmares of the road traffic accident four months later: she would get out of bed distressed and insist on sleeping with her parents. Cecilia mentioned these ongoing difficulties to her health visitor, who suggested that if Abigail could sort out the story of the accident in the day-time, then it would not play on her mind at night. Specifically Cecilia was advised to have a special time when Abigail came home from school in which she could crayon, draw or paint about the accident and to show interest in what she produced. Unfortunately Cecilia upset Abigail with her first drawing because she drew their car nearly hitting a house rather than a motorway bridge, and suggesting that Abigail draw it properly, at which Abigail had a tantrum. After which Cecilia realised she must not take over Abigail's artwork but simply raise interesting questions such as 'Are you going to draw the bridge today?' or 'Are you going to draw how you are better now?' Abigail continued with her artwork for about two weeks before declaring she was bored with it, by which time there was a notable decrease in the frequency of nightmares, though they did temporarily increase in frequency in the first few days of drawing and painting.

Cecilia attended a Group Parent Training Programme to help address her concerns about Abigail and Anthony. At the first session the group leader talked about ignoring children's temper tantrums. Cecilia recognised that she used to do this before the road traffic accident but now found that she got hooked into the children's tantrums in the hope of quickly dispelling them, then when this didn't work she would rave, leading to an intensification of the tantrums. It struck a chord with her when the group leader said children enjoy attention even if it is for bad things and that she was unwittingly giving them a reward (attention) for bad behaviour, which would increase the latter. Cecilia planned to ignore the temper tantrums of Anthony and Abigail and as she had been taught to expect, the tantrums increased in frequency and intensity as they both felt they were losing control of her. However, she found it very difficult to ignore Abigail when she accused her of not loving her as much as Anthony. Cecilia took these concerns to the next group session and though she quickly realised that Abigail's accusation was bait to gain attention, she had lingering doubts that maybe Abigail did not feel loved.

The main focus of the next session was on praise, catching your child being good and praising the particulars of what they have just done. Cecilia realised that since the accident, with the exception of reading a story at bedtime, she noticed Abigail only when she was being naughty, usually involving fighting with Anthony. Cecilia decided to make a concerted effort to track Abigail's good behaviour and comment very specifically on it, e.g. 'That's good, you have put your shoes in the cupboard'. She had learnt in the session that general praise, e.g. 'You have been a good girl today', was much less effective because the child would not connect it with a particular behaviour and would probably simply take it that Mum was in a good mood. Cecilia further realised that since the accident, Abigail was subjected to a constant barrage of her criticisms and that for any criticism to be taken seriously it had to be given in an overall context of praise. As the group leader put it, the 'black' had to be contrasted with the 'white' to be visible. What Cecilia found particularly distressing were the fights between Anthony and Abigail, which usually took place around bedtime. Typically Abigail would wind Anthony up and he would respond by biting her. Cecilia suspected that this behaviour occurred because neither of them wanted to go to bed following the accident and were afraid of flashbacks or dreams. In the Group Parent Training Programme she learnt a procedure called time out that she could apply when they fought. In the event of a fight Abigail and Anthony were sent to separate naughty corners with nothing to do at all (time out from rewarding behaviour) for a few minutes and allowed out only when Cecilia said so. While Cecilia could see the attraction of the strategy in that the one thing her children hated was boredom, in practice it was more difficult to apply. First of all she discovered that from the two corners she had selected, the two childen could in fact just about see each other and would amuse themselves quietly pulling faces at each other as she sat with her back to them. Once she realised this, she changed the location of Abigail's corner but then she became tearful and reverted to mumbling, 'You don't really love me', which upset Cecilia. She found it difficult to ignore these utterances but remained insistent that Abigail would be allowed out only when she had been quiet for a few minutes. Anthony was refusing to go to his naughty corner now that his sister was not in sight. She enlisted the help of her husband Dave to take Anthony to the naughty corner despite his screams, and to hold his arms by his side, simply repeating that he would not be allowed out until he had been quiet awhile. During the time out procedure Dave did not make eye contact with Anthony or respond in any way to his verbalisations. After two to three weeks the disruptive behaviour before bedtime ceased.

Adolescent

Adolescent males will often under-report any psychological distress in the wake of a trauma as part of being macho. However, friends and family may notice increased irritability, moodiness and poor concentration, but may be unsure whether this is to do with the trauma or marks the onset of typical adolescent behaviour. Sometimes there may be other negative life events, such as parents splitting up, that better account for the seeming personality change than the trauma.

While female adolescents do not usually under-report symptoms, it can be difficult to distinguish typical adolescent concerns from what might be termed psychopathology.

Cecilia's elder daughter, 14-year-old Amanda, had four sutures put in her cheek after the accident, leaving a small scar. Cecilia did not think there was anything abnormal about Amanda's concerns in the first three months after the accident but by six months she began thinking that her response was excessive. Matters came to a head when Cecilia discovered that Amanda had been lying to get out of swimming and sports lessons in school. When Cecilia confronted Amanda about this, she broke down in tears and said, 'The others will be able to tell I am ugly'. Cecilia decided to use her 'dares' approach to this and suggested to Amanda that she dare herself just to go to a swimming class and test out her theory whether anyone will think her ugly. Amanda protested that she knew they would and Cecilia said that she was prepared to bet her they would not, but neither would really know the truth until she conducted the experiment. In the event there were no negative comments from Amanda's peers and she proceeded to dare herself to engage in sports lessons. Though Amanda continued to insist on wearing lots of make-up socially, Cecilia regarded this as little more than adolescent self-consciousness.

Cecilia also tried to get Amanda to apply the 'dare' strategy to not getting out of bed to check that doors were locked and appliances were switched off, but she felt unable to do this. When Cecilia quizzed her over this Amanda reluctantly explained, 'It's like a voice in my head telling me I have just got to, it is my responsibility if anything goes wrong', and she suggested telling the voice to 'Take a hike, the way you do some of the boys in school'. Cecilia also explained that half the responsibility for house security was hers, and the other half was her Dad's, and that left no slice of the responsibility pie for Amanda.

The strategies Cecilia used with her children were carefully matched to their age. Techniques and language used with young people with similar difficulties have to be carefully adapted to the developmental age of the child or adolescent.

13

Justice

In the immediate aftermath of an extreme trauma, thoughts of seeking compensation are likely to be far from your mind. But as time passes, friends and relatives are likely to increasingly raise the issue. You may then seek legal advice but have very mixed feelings: on the one hand you are pleased that you are seeking justice but the litigation process, making a statement, answering solicitor's queries and so on act as painful reminders of the trauma. Matters are often not helped by a relative or friend asking about the progress of the compensation claim, in such a way as to imply that the trauma is no more than a useful way of your making money. The upshot is that many trauma victims pursue litigation with ambivalent feelings. On a more positive note, via litigation, you can get the psychological and/or physical help you need usually much more quickly than relying on the NHS. For example NHS waiting lists for cognitive behavioural therapy (the evidence-based approach described in this book) are typically from six to eighteen months whereas it is possible to be referred privately to an accredited cognitive behavioural therapist (see the website of the British Association for Behavioural and Cognitive Psychotherapies www.babcp.com) usually within weeks following recommendation by an expert witness, who would usually be a psychologist or psychiatrist.

The legal journey

In the first instance solicitors usually instruct a generalist expert witness, typically a GP, to prepare a report and if significant psychological problems are identified, recommendation is made for the definitive opinion of a psychologist or psychiatrist. The waiting time for a specialist appointment is typically one to three months and a report is usually produced within a couple of weeks. The defendant's solicitors may delay appointing their own specialist expert witness until after they have seen the report of the first expert. Obviously seeing the defendant's specialist expert does delay matters further and is an added stress; however, in some instances the defendant's and claimant's solicitors appoint one jointly agreed expert. Under court rules an expert's duty is to the court and not their instructing solicitor, that is they are required to give an objective view of the trauma and its effects on the claimant.

It is not possible to conclude litigation until it is known with some certainty how you are likely to be psychologically and physically in the long term. As a rough rule of thumb, if an expert witness has identified psychological and/or physical problems, they are unlikely to make a definitive prognosis in under two years. The litigation can be further drawn out because the expert witness recommends a particular treatment or operation and wishes to defer making a prognosis until afterwards. Litigation may be drawn out even further if there is disagreement between the expert witness instructed on behalf of the claimant and the expert witness instructed on behalf of the defendant. The two experts are then asked to produce a joint statement for the court indicating the points they agree on and those they disagree on and giving their reasons. Thus the apparent slow pace of the legal process is by no means wholly in the control of the legal profession. Nevertheless the protracted nature of the proceedings can take its toll emotionally and at a time when you are ill equipped to cope with the added stress.

Many litigants are haunted by the fear of having to give evidence in court but the good news is that this happens in only a small proportion of cases: the vast majority of cases are settled out of court. However, it is impossible to be certain at the outset which cases will involve attendance at court: it depends in part on how great the level of disagreement between the experts is. Sometimes agreements are not reached between the defendant's and claimant's solicitors until the parties are in the court building.

Cecilia was terrified at the prospect of initiating litigation and protested to her policeman husband, Dave, that she just wanted to forget about the accident. She played a horror video of standing in the dock in court, being cross-examined, her mind going blank, and bursting into tears. Dave consoled her with the thought that if such a scenario did unfold, it would speak volumes for her distress since the trauma. However, she became angry at this and accused him angrily, 'So you are saying I should put on a show!' Dave had become practised at not rising to the bait of Cecilia's irritability and replied, 'All you have to do is be yourself'. But she retorted, 'It is all right for you, you are a policeman'. Dave replied that he would see if he could get someone from the Witness Support Service (which operates in criminal matters, e.g. cases of assault, such as Kevin's) to acquaint her with an empty court one lunchtime or failing that her solicitor might do the same.

Litigation stress

The stress of litigation is sometimes expressed in delaying replying to solicitor's letters or phone calls and sometimes being unable to face opening letters, letting them pile up if no one else is available to open them. While litigants understandably look forward to the end of litigation, there is no evidence that their diagnostic status changes (see for example a study by Blanchard and Hickling (1997) of road traffic accident victims), that is, if you were say suffering from PTSD at the end of litigation, the likelihood is that you would probably continue to suffer from it afterwards. Thus from a psychological point of view, the end of the legal process changes very little, even though you are likely to feel mightily relieved that it is over.

Patrick discovered that the defendant's solicitors had arranged video surveillance of him. Patrick felt that this was an invasion of his privacy and implied he was lying about his incapacity since his fall from the roof. Matters were compounded when part of the video showed him getting out of his car and going into the hospice to see his dying friend Paul, then leaving the premises an hour later. Patrick felt that the video represented a gross intrusion. His solicitor calmed him slightly by asking, 'How can the insurers, who do not know you from Adam, be sure a person is not trying to pull the wool over their eyes?' but acknowledged that surveillance targeting a hospice was particularly tasteless. Since learning of the video Patrick was constantly looking over his shoulder and felt he was being viewed literally and metaphorically as a criminal. His disquiet increased when the defendant's expert psychiatrist used the video as evidence that he was not clinically depressed. However, he was consoled a little when his solicitor's expert psychologist pointed out that observable behaviour per se, such as contained in a video, is not part of the diagnostic criteria for depression and has little relevance to his psychological state. Nevertheless he was left feeling that he just wanted the whole matter of litigation over and done with as soon as possible.

Previous difficulties

An expert witness is unlikely to be prepared to give a definitive opinion on the effects of your trauma without inspecting your GP and hospital records. At interview the expert will have asked you about any previous psychological difficulties, drink or drug problems, abuse as a child, family psychiatric history, criminal behaviour or other major negative life events. If there is a significant gap between what you say and what is in the records, the expert will raise questions in the report about your reliability and may go as far as to suggest you are malingering, i.e. deliberately exaggerating symptoms for the sake of financial gain. It should be remembered that although an expert may have been instructed by your solicitor, it is not like being the expert's patient. The duty of the expert is simply to inform the court of your symptoms and the likely explanation (causation). The expert has to separate out the effects of other major negative life events from the effects of the trauma for which compensation is being sought.

Karen was outraged when the expert asked her whether she

had been abused as a child: she protested that this was an intrusion of her privacy and she was seeing him because of the effect of her partner's rapes. The expert explained to Karen that if very bad things had happened to her as a child, it would make it easier to understand why she might have a very strong reaction to bad things in adulthood, thus if a trauma is not put into the overall context of a person's life it may be seen as an overreaction. Reluctantly Karen told the expert about the sexual abuse by her cousin from age 6 to 12. After the one and a half-hour appointment with the expert, she felt totally drained for the rest of the day and had nightmares of both the abuse and the rapes that night. On waking she was afraid to close her eyes for fear of her nightmare recurring. Fortunately the expert's report for the Criminal Injuries Compensation Authority recommended she undergo cognitive behavioural therapy and she used some of her award to fund treatment.

Disagreeing with an expert's report

Your solicitor will usually ask you for any comments on an expert's report shortly after receiving it. Sometimes the expert has got a matter of fact wrong, such as the date or location of the accident, and via the solicitor these matters are easily righted. It is much more difficult if the expert's opinion is that some other event is largely responsible for your current problems or that they are simply an exacerbation of pre-existing difficulties or that you are exaggerating your problems. Such 'alternative' explanations may make you feel angry, particularly so if the expert had been abrupt at interview or not allowed you to explain yourself properly. However, it is important to let your solicitor know what you disagree with in the expert's report and why. Under the Civil Procedure Rules the solicitor can then put in writing questions to the expert that he or she is obliged to respond to within a specified time period. If you have seen experts instructed by both sides, it is not uncommon for them to disagree on matters of diagnosis, causation or malingering.

John's father died suddenly six months before his involvement in the gas explosion. John had been very close to him and he visited his GP on two occasions for sick notes because he felt that he could not cope with his grief and the pressure of work. On the second occasion his GP prescribed antidepressants but fearful of dependence on them, John did not take them. John was outraged when one of the experts concluded that the gas explosion had simply exacerbated his previous depression. He felt that the other expert more accurately described his difficulties, identifying a bereavement reaction that lasted for two months after his father's death but serving to make him more vulnerable than others to the effect of any subsequent trauma. This expert concluded that he suffered from PTSD and depression following the gas explosion and that on the balance of probability he would recover within six months, but if he failed to improve he would need cognitive behavioural therapy. The other expert did not agree that CBT was necessary, but John's solicitor applied for and received an interim payment to fund treatment. Given the great gulf in opinion and with the prospect of court looming, his solicitor arranged a meeting with a barrister in chambers. At this meeting John, his solicitor and their own expert witness would also be present to discuss the other expert's response to questions they had raised about his report. Before this meeting took place the defendant's insurers increased the size of their offer; John's solicitor advised him that the defendant's barrister had probably seen the inadequacy of their own expert's reply and in an effort to avoid losing in court had made a more realistic offer. John decided to take the offer (which was technically 'paid into court'), rather than run the risk of a judge awarding a smaller sum than that having been 'paid into court' and thereby having to suffer the penalty of paying the legal fees of both sides involved in the dispute.

The anti-climax

Many trauma victims pursue litigation in the belief that they will get justice and indeed the head of steam created by their anger fuels the legal journey.

John, who suffered PTSD and depression from a gas explosion at work, was incensed that his managers tried to pin the blame on him and his colleague, Alan. It was not until twelve months after the explosion that his employer's solicitors accepted liability for the explosion, acknowledging that certain gaskets were long overdue for replacement and this only after investigation by the Health and Safety Executive. John was frustrated that there was still no personal apology from his managers; their response was still of the form, 'If you do not like the heat in the kitchen get out' and they tried to make him use his own time in which to attend cognitive behavioural therapy. Under pressure from his solicitors, John's employer did allow him time off for treatment, but only when it was suggested a judge might take a dim view of doing otherwise and this may affect quantum (the amount of damages John was awarded). John very much wanted his 'day in court' to right the wrongs perpetrated by his employer. He was disappointed to learn that in the unlikely event of the case reaching court, probably only a representative of the defendant's insurers would be present, and that this person would have no personal knowledge of him, would not deal in apologies, and would seek to part with as little money as possible. In the event the case was settled out of court and he received a cheque through the post from his solicitor. He showed his wife the cheque and in disbelief said, 'Is that it then?' She replied, 'What did you expect, a bolt of lightning?' John mused that all the legal process does is to translate distress into a sum of money and no amount of money could compensate him for what he had been through. His wife commented: 'It's like sending a neighbour a bouquet of flowers when they have lost a loved one: it doesn't bring the dead person back but it is the best you can do'. John agreed that it was 'something' but not the justice he yearned for. The conclusion of the case was for him a great anti-climax.

14

Getting further help

While there are in theory very effective treatments for the whole spectrum of post trauma responses, in practice provision is poor, with NHS psychology waiting lists typically six to eighteen months. To compound matters further, unreliable diagnosis (see Appendix B) is commonplace, making for poorly targeted treatment both within and outside the NHS.

Angela had been treated unsuccessfully for ten years by the NHS psychiatric/psychological services, including cognitive behavioural therapy, for 'depression'. While indeed she was clinically depressed, she had a long history of physical and sexual abuse in childhood and adolescence and she experienced distressing intrusions of these events, meeting diagnostic criteria for post-traumatic stress disorder. She was greatly relieved that the more comprehensive diagnosis opened up new treatment options.

No self-help book can be a substitute for professional help, but when the latter is not forthcoming, this book may help you start on the road to 'finding me again'. It can also make you more psychologically sophisticated and empower you to challenge both the diagnoses and treatments of professionals.

In Chapter 4 the evidence-based treatments for post trauma responses were identified as cognitive behavioural therapy and EMDR. Accredited cognitive behavioural therapists may be found at the website of the British Association for Behavioural and Cognitive Psychotherapies (BABCP) www.babcp.com or EMDR therapists at www.emdrassociation.org.uk

GP

In the wake of a trauma the first port of call is often the GP, particularly so if there are associated physical injuries. The GP is likely to regard report of psychological symptoms in the couple of months after the trauma as a natural response given the extremity of the trauma, referring only as far as the practice or Primary Care Trust counsellor in this period. Given that most people who suffer from a disorder such as PTSD do recover of their own accord within the year, the GP's 'wait and see' approach is not an unreasonable response. Further the GP may be reluctant to refer on to secondary care (where a consultant psychiatrist is usually the gatekeeper to services) because of the long waiting list for psychological services, offering antidepressants for those most troubled and/or a hypnotic agent (e.g. Zopiclone) for those with persistent and pronounced sleep difficulties. Sometimes trauma victims are frustrated by the GP asking, 'What do you want me to do?', believing that the GP is supposed to be the expert, but in this context as far as the psychological symptoms are concerned the GP can act only as a signpost and provide some limited support, normalising symptoms.

Occupational health service

If the trauma has happened in the context of the workplace, employers, particularly the larger ones such as banks, bus operators, police or major manufacturers, will usually facilitate access to counselling via an occupational health service, but they may not be aware of the need for the practitioner to be an accredited therapist. The major benefit of occupational health service referral is that referral to a specialist is much quicker than in the NHS. However, the employee may be angry at the employer for a number of reasons: blaming him or her after the trauma, making infrequent contact while off work, making contact that has been unsympathetic or even threatening, setting inappropriate milestones for a return to work. A therapist funded by the employer will have to take any anger seriously and liaise appropriately with the occupational health service and thereby the employer.

Defendant's insurers

It may also be possible to expedite treatment if the defendant's insurers agree to fund it. From the insurer's point of view the quicker you get better, the less they have to pay in compensation. The worst scenario from the insurer's perspective is the claimant who does not recover and is permanently unable to work. In such cases, particularly if the person is young, the loss of earnings may be huge. However, the insurers may not fund treatment if their own expert does not deem it appropriate. Sometimes expert witnesses disagree on the need for treatment (or the number of sessions required); treatment can nevertheless be funded by seeking an interim payment via your solicitor if liability has already been agreed.

Criminal Injuries Compensation Authority (CICA)

If you are the victim of a crime, you may seek compensation via the CICA and part of the award can be earmarked for cognitive behavioural treatment. You could then seek out an accredited therapist via the BABCP website. The CICA application is probably best made via a solicitor, who can also handle appeals against decisions and awards made.

Agencies

Counsellors are becoming increasingly acquainted with cognitive behavioural approaches and many work for charities (in voluntary and non-voluntary capacities), with waiting lists much shorter than the NHS. Those traumatised in the Armed Services may seek CBT at one of the three residential facilities of the charity, Combat Stress (www.combatstress.org.uk). In some areas charities liaise with NHS Primary Care Trusts to provide services and are partly funded by them. However, the charities are locally based and in some areas there is no provision. It is unlikely that the counsellor will be an accredited cognitive behavioural psychotherapist (see www.babcp.com website) but this is not to say that they will not be sufficiently aware of a CBT approach to make a significant difference.

There are national agencies for specific populations such as the Victim Support Service (www.victimsupport.org), but this agency provides support rather than specific counselling. Social support is an important predictor of likelihood of recovery from trauma, groups devoted to the needs of specific population can lessen the sense of isolation and can be a useful adjunct to therapy.

An extreme trauma raises in graphic form existential questions about meaning and human suffering, and it is no longer possible to be too busy to address such difficult questions. While there are no easy answers, most religious traditions have grappled with these problems and a sympathetic cleric is unlikely to give a trite or pat answer to your concerns and may be a pathway to a supportive community.

Guidance for professionals using this book

This self-help book complements *Counselling for Post-Traumatic Stress Disorder* (3rd edition, Scott and Stradling 2006). When clients first arrive for counselling, their feelings are often mixed. On the one hand they are relieved that at last help might be forthcoming and on the other hand they reproach themselves that it should have come to this, 'baring your soul to a total stranger'. Because the counselling offered is most usually individual, it can implicitly underline a client's belief in their 'oddness'. This self-help book serves as an antidote to the client's sense of isolation. Most traumatised clients will be able to identify with one or more of the case examples and will at least get their bearings on the directions they might go. The counsellor's task is to provide detailed directions and sustenance for the journey, recruiting where possible significant others as quasi-therapists in the community.

Chapters 1–4 of this book provide the client with an orientation to the treatment programme, developing the client's psychological sophistication. Without an awareness of the earlier chapters, there is a danger that the client will see the techniques detailed in subsequent chapters as a random assembly of strategies and of no more significance to those advocated by any passing pedlar of psychological wares. It is recommended that the client is asked to read the first couple of chapters as a homework assignment after the first session. Further, if at all possible the client should share their readings with someone significant in their lives, ideally asking them also to read Chapters 1–4. The agenda for the second treatment session should include a review of the reading material and problem-solving of any difficulties, for example the counsellor may clarify a point of the text not understood or help the client refine their reading in the light of their concentration problems.

The focus of Chapter 5 is on the trauma victim's avoidance of reminders of their trauma and potentially uplifting activities. The narrative is one of living in the land of avoidance rather than the land of approach and of taking gradual steps to reverse this. It is recommended that clients are asked to read Chapter 5 after the second session and to discuss its contents at the third session. The contents of Chapter 5 provide a springboard for the therapist and client, distilling homework assignments that are in effect forays into the land of approach. Any problems with these forays are discussed at the fourth session and new goals elaborated. The client should be advised to read Chapter 5 again as a reference, so that the book not only helps to structure therapy sessions but also is recast as a survival manual that may be used in the event of difficulties after therapy has finished. The review of avoidance and steps taken to overcome it should be an integral part of all subsequent counselling sessions.

The main thrust of Chapter 6 is the redundancy of blocking the traumatic memory and the insidious effects of ruminating about it. The inadequacy of these strategies should be a major focus of the fifth session. A range of alternative coping strategies are presented in Chapter 6 and it is suggested that in order to enhance the therapeutic relationship the least painful strategies are tried first. It is suggested that Chapter 6 should be given as a homework assignment after the fifth session. Once again at the next session its contents and the first practical steps to implement it should be discussed.

The cognitive contextual approach described in this volume and the accompanying *Counselling for Post-Traumatic Stress Disorder* (Scott and Stradling 2006) differs from the traditional cognitive behavioural approach in that there is an additional emphasis on restoring relationships. This departure is justified theoretically because social support has been found to be the major predictor of the resolution of post trauma symptoms. While it remains to be demonstrated empirically whether there is a significant added value in including this extra component, my experience is that it greatly facilitates treatment. It is recommended that the materials in Chapter 7 are woven into the fabric of sessions from the second session onwards.

Traumatic memory is an emotional memory and as such it may be accessed in a negative mood state. Once the traumatic memory is accessed it is likely to be the focus of rumination. The triggers for the negative mood state are not necessarily related to the trauma and a broad ranging approach to managing mood is therefore necessary and detailed in Chapter 8. This chapter should be discussed in about the sixth session and the client asked to read it as a homework assignment. In the following session the client's attempts at the MOOD records are reviewed.

Chapters 9–11 are devoted to particular saboteurs of managing mood (pain, sleep, previous trauma). How much of this material will be addressed in the seventh session onwards depends on which saboteurs are operative for a particular client. These chapters allow the counsellor to fine tune the treatment programme to the needs of a particular client. While it is the case, as detailed in Chapter 4, that it is manualised treatments for post trauma responses that have been found to have demonstrated efficacy, it is doubtful that a wholly standardised approach would be effective with the typical multiple problem client found in routine clinical practice (and often excluded from controlled trials). Chapters 5–11 strike a balance between a standardised approach and a wholly idiosyncratic response to a trauma victim's difficulties.

It is important that children and adolescents are not regarded and treated as simply young adults. The presentation of trauma symptoms in young people is often different from that of their adult counterparts. In Chapter 12 developmentally appropriate treatment strategies are described. Finally, Chapters 13 and 14 discuss the advantages and disadvantages of different vehicles for restoring a sense of 'me' again.

This book can also be used as a discussion text for groups of trauma victims undergoing treatment. It is recommended that the groups are homogenous, e.g. a road traffic accident group or adult survivors of sexual abuse. The likelihood is that group members will identify with one or more of the prototypical illustrative cases, promoting discussions in which the less articulate group member is not disadvantaged. In identifying with a particular case, homework options are made explicit and can be negotiated in the group. The group has the added advantage of providing support.

Appendix A: Screening for PTSD

In Chapter 1 the Trauma Screening Questionnaire (Brewin et al. 2002) was introduced and is reproduced here.

Table A.1 **Trauma Screening Questionnaire**

Your Own Reactions Now to the Traumatic Event
Please consider the following reactions that sometimes occur after a traumatic event. This questionnaire is concerned with your personal reactions to the traumatic event. Please indicate whether or not you have experienced any of the following AT LEAST TWICE IN THE PAST WEEK:

	Yes, at least twice in the past week	No
1 Upsetting thoughts or memories about the event that have come into your mind against your will		
2 Upsetting dreams about the event		
3 Acting or feeling as though the event were happening again		
4 Feeling upset by reminder of the event		
5 Bodily reactions (such as fast heartbeat, stomach churning, sweatiness, dizziness) when reminded of the event		

	Yes, at least twice in the past week	No
6 Difficulty falling or staying asleep		
7 Irritability or outbursts of anger		
8 Difficulty concentrating		
9 Heightened awareness of potential danger to yourself and others		
10 Being jumpy or being startled at something unexpected		

If you have answered six or more with a 'yes' then it is likely, but by no means guaranteed, that you are suffering from PTSD. Brewin and colleagues (2002) had survivors of the Ladbroke Grove train crash complete the TSQ and compared the results with the findings of a standardised clinical interview. Of the people who marked 'yes' to six or more items on the TSQ, 86 per cent were found to have PTSD when assessed by a structured clinical interview, whereas of the people who marked 'yes' to fewer than six questions, only 7 per cent met criteria for PTSD. Similar results were obtained on a separate sample of assault victims. More recently the TSQ has been used to screen survivors of the London bombings of 7 July 2005. Of those completing it about one-quarter have been referred on further professional help. Your results on the TSQ need careful checking out by a competent mental health professional using the standardised type of clinical interview used by Brewin and colleagues.

Appendix B: Unreliable diagnosis

In a standardised interview the assessor asks questions about each of the symptoms that comprise the diagnostic criteria for a disorder (see Appendix C for the American Psychiatric Association's DSM-IV-TR diagnostic criteria for PTSD, depression and panic disorder) and there are published guidelines as to whether on the basis of all the information available that symptom is considered present. If a standardised interview is not used then the reliability is between 32 and 54 per cent (Beck et al. 1962) but with a standardised structured interview the level of agreement (termed reliability) is about 90 per cent, i.e. nine out of ten assessors would come to the same conclusion about the diagnosis. While standardised structured interviews are almost always used for research purposes, they are time consuming and rarely used in routine practice, making for misdiagnosis which in turn may lead to inappropriate treatment. In a major study comparing standardised interviews with routine open-ended interviews, in the latter 50 per cent of PTSD cases were missed (Zimmerman and Mattia 1999). The danger of the commonplace open-ended clinical interview is that the assessor tends to stop at the first disorder they identify (Zimmerman and Mattia 1999) resulting in poorly targeted treatment. The failure to incorporate a standardised clinical interview in the assessment can also lead to unreliable diagnosis when people are seeking compensation (Scott and Sembi 2002) and with regard to treatment (Scott and Sembi 2006).

Appendix C: DSM-IV-TR diagnostic criteria for PTSD, depression and panic disorder

DSM-IV-TR diagnostic criteria for PTSD

A The person has been exposed to the traumatic events in which both of the following were present:

1 The person experienced, witnessed or was confronted with an event or events that involved actual or threatened death or serious injuries, or a threat to the physical integrity of self or others.

2 The person's response involved intense fear, helplessness or horror. Note: in children, this may be expressed instead by a disorganised or agitated behaviour.

B The traumatic events is consistently re-experienced in one (or more) of the following ways:

1 Recurrent and intrusive distressing recollections of the events, including images, thoughts, or perceptions. Note: in young children, repetitive play may occur in which themes or aspects of the trauma are expressed.

2 Recurrent distressing dreams of the event. Note: in children, there may be frightening dreams without recognisable content.

3 Acting or feeling as if the traumatic event were

recurring (includes a sense of reliving the experience, illusions, hallucinations and dissociative flashback episodes, including those that occur on awakening or when intoxicated). Note: in young children trauma specific re-enactment may occur.

4   Intense psychological distress at exposure to internal or external cues that symbolise or resemble an aspect of the traumatic event.

5   Physiological reactivity on exposure to internal or external cues that symbolise or resemble an aspect of the traumatic event.

C Persistent avoidance of stimuli associated with the trauma and numbing of general responsiveness (not present before the trauma), as indicated by three (or more) of the following:

1   Efforts to avoid thoughts, feelings or conversations associated with the trauma.

2   Efforts to avoid activities, places or people that arouse recollections of the trauma.

3   Inability to recall an important aspect of the trauma.

4   Markedly diminished interest or participation in significance activities.

5   Feeling of detachment or estrangement from others.

6   Restricted range of affect (e.g. unable to have loving feelings).

7   Sense of a foreshortened future (e.g. does not expect to have a career, marriage, children, or a normal life span).

D Persistent symptoms of increased arousal (not present before the trauma), as indicated by two (or more) of the following:

1   Difficulty falling or staying asleep.

2   Irritability or outbursts of anger.

3   Difficulty concentrating.

4   Hypervigilance.

5   Exaggerated startle response.

E Duration of the disturbance (symptoms in criteria B, C and D) is more than one month.

F The disturbance causes clinically significant distress or impairment in social, occupational or other important areas of functioning.

Specify if:

Acute: if duration of symptoms is less than three months.

Chronic: if duration of symptoms is three months or more.

There is a footnote to the criteria (p. 465 of the DSM-IV-TR) which states that additional symptoms (see next section) may occur and are more commonly seen in association with interpersonal stressors such as childhood physical/sexual abuse or domestic battering.

Possible additional symptoms associated with PTSD

1 Impaired affect modulation – an inability to moderate emotional 'weather' and behaviour.
2 Self-destructive and impulsive behaviour.
3 Dissociative symptoms – some degree of loss of awareness of surroundings.
4 Somatic complaints – bodily expressions of emotional distress.
5 Feelings of ineffectiveness, shame, despair or hopelessness.
6 Feeling permanently damaged.
7 A loss of previously sustained beliefs.
8 Hostility.
9 Social withdrawal.
10 Feeling constantly threatened.
11 Impaired relationship with others.
12 A change from the individual's previous personality characteristics.

DSM-IV-TR diagnostic criteria for depression

A Five (or more) of the following symptoms have been present during the same two-week period and represent a change from previous functioning; at least one of the symptoms is either (1) depressed mood or (2) loss of interest or pleasure.

1   Depressed mood most of the day, nearly every day, as indicated by either subjective reports (e.g. feels sad or empty) or observation made by others (e.g. appears tearful). Note: in children and adolescents can be irritable mood.

2   Markedly diminished interest or pleasure in all, or almost all, activities most of the day, nearly every day (as indicated by either subjective account or observation made by others).

3   Significant weight loss when not dieting or weight gain (e.g. a change of more than 5 per cent of body weight in a month) or decrease or increase in appetite nearly every day. Note: in children, consider failure to make expected weight gains.

4   Insomnia or hypersomnia nearly every day.

5   Psychomotor agitation or retardation nearly every day (observable by others, not merely subjective feelings of restlessness or being slowed down).

6   Fatigue or loss of energy nearly every day.

7   Feelings of worthlessness or excessive or inappropriate guilt (which may be delusional) nearly every day (not merely self-reproach or guilt about being sick).

8   Diminished ability to think or concentrate or indecisiveness, nearly every day (either by subjective account or as observed by others).

9   Recurrent thoughts of death (not just fear of dying), recurrent suicidal ideation without a specific plan, or a suicide attempt or a specific plan for committing suicide.

B The symptoms do not meet criteria for a Mixed Episode (Manic Episode and Major Depressive Episode).

C The symptoms cause clinically significant distress or impairment in social, occupational, or other important areas of functioning.

D The symptoms are not due to the direct physiological

effects of a substance (e.g. a drug of abuse) or a general medical condition (e.g. hypothyroidism).

E The symptoms are not better accounted for by bereavement, i.e after the loss of a loved one, the symptoms persist for longer than two months.

DSM-IV-TR diagnostic criteria for panic disorder

A: both (1) and (2)

1   Recurrent unexpected panic attacks – a discrete period of intense fear or discomfort, in which four (or more) of the following symptoms developed abruptly and reached a peak within ten minutes:

- palpitations, pounding heart, or accelerated heart rate
- sweating
- trembling or shaking
- sensations of shortness of breath or smothering
- feeling of choking
- chest pain or discomfort
- nausea or abdominal distress
- feeling dizzy, unsteady, light-headed or faint
- derealisation (feeling of unreality) or depersonalisation (being detached from oneself)
- fear of losing control or going crazy
- fear of dying
- paresthesias (numbness or tingling sensations)
- chills or hot flushes.

2   At least one of the attacks has been followed by one month (or more) of one (or more) of the following:

- persistent concern about having additional attacks
- worry about the implications of the attack or its consequences (e.g. losing control, having a heat attack, 'going crazy')
- a significant change in behaviour related to the attacks

Note: Panic disorder may occur with or without agoraphobia.

DSM-IV-TR diagnostic criteria for agoraphobia

A Anxiety about being in places or situations from which escape might be difficult (or embarrassing) or in which help may not be available in the event of having an unexpected or situationally predisposed panic attack or panic-like symptoms. Agoraphobic fears typically involve characteristic clusters of situations that include being outside the home alone, being in a crowd or standing in a line, being on a bridge, and travelling in a bus, train or car.

B The situations are avoided (e.g. travel is restricted) or else are endured with marked distress or with anxiety about having a panic attack or panic-like symptoms, or require the presence of a companion.

References

Alford, B.A. and Beck, A.T. (1997) *The Integrative Power of Cognitive Therapy*. New York: Guilford Press.

American Psychiatric Association (APA) (2000) *Diagnostic and Statistical Manual of Mental Disorders, Fourth Edition, Text Revision* (DSM-IV-TR). Washington, DC: APA.

Amir, M., Kaplan, Z., Neumann, L., Sharabani, R. and Shani, N. (1997) Post-traumatic stress disorder, tenderness and fibromyalgia. *Journal of Psychosomatic Research*, 42: 607–613.

Beck, A.T., Ward, C.H., Mendelson, M., Mock, J.E. and Erbaugh, J.K. (1962) Reliability of psychiatric diagnoses: A study of consistency of clinical judgements and ratings. *American Journal of Psychiatry*, 119: 351–357.

Becker, C.B., Zayfert, C. and Anderson, E. (2004) A survey of psychologists' attitudes towards and utilization of exposure therapy for PTSD. *Behaviour Research and Therapy*, 42: 277–292.

Blanchard, E.B. and Hickling, E. (1997) *After the Crash: Assessment and Treatment of Motor Vehicle Accidents Survivors*. Washington, DC: American Psychological Association.

Bradley, R., Greene, J., Russ, E., Dutra, L. and Westen, D. (2005) A multidimensional meta-analysis of psychotherapy for PTSD. *American Journal of Psychiatry*, 162: 214–228.

Breslau, N., Davis, G.C., Andreski, P. and Peterson, E. (1991) Traumatic events and post-traumatic stress disorder in an urban population of young adults. *Archives of General Psychiatry*, 48: 216–222.

Brewin, C.R., Andrews, B. and Valentine, J.D. (2000) Meta-analysis of risk factors for post-traumatic stress disorder in trauma exposed adults. *Journal of Consulting and Clinical Psychology*, 68: 748–766.

Brewin, C.R., Rose, S. and Andrews, B. (2002) A brief screening instrument for post-traumatic stress disorder. *British Journal of Psychiatry*, 181: 158–162.

Brown, T.A., Campbell, L.A. and Lehman, C.L. (2001) Current and lifetime comorbidity of the DSM IV anxiety and mood disorders in a large clinical sample. *Journal of Abnormal Psychology*, 110: 585–599.

Butler, A.C., Chapman, J.E., Forman, E.M. and Beck, A.T. (2006) The empirical status of cognitive-behavioural therapy: A review of meta-analyses. *Clinical Psychology Review*, 26: 17–31.

Chapman, R.A., Shedlack, K.J. and France, J. (2006) Stop-Think-Relax: An adapted self-control training strategy for individuals with mental retardation and coexisting psychiatric illness. *Cognitive and Behavioural Practice*, 13: 205–214.

Dunmore, E., Clark, D.M. and Ehlers, A. (1999) Cognitive factors involved in the onset and maintenance of post-traumatic stress disorder after physical or sexual assault. *Behaviour Research and Therapy*, 37: 809–829.

Dunmore, E., Clark, D.M. and Ehlers, A. (2001) A prospective investigation of the role of cognitive factors in persistent post-traumatic stress disorder after physical or sexual assault. *Behaviour Research and Therapy*, 39: 1063–1084.

Foa, E.B. and Rothbaum, B.O. (1998) *Treating the Trauma of Rape*. New York: Guilford Press.

Goleman, D. (1996) *Emotional Intelligence: Why It Can Matter More than IQ*. London: Bloomsbury.

Hayes, S.C., Strosahl, K.D. and Wilson, K.G. (1999) *Acceptance and Commitment Therapy: An Experiential Approach to Behaviour Change*. New York: Guilford Press.

Hubbard, J., Realmuto, G.M., Northwood, A.K. and Masten, A.S. (1995) Co-morbidity of psychiatric diagnoses with post-traumatic stress disorder in survivors of childhood trauma. *Journal of the American Academy of Child and Adolescent Psychiatry*, 34: 1167–1173.

Jaycox, L.H., Foa, E.B. and Morral, A.R. (1998) Influence of emotional engagement and habituation on exposure therapy for PTSD. *Journal of Consulting and Clinical Psychology*, 66: 185–192.

LeDoux, J.E. (1998) *The Emotional Brain: The Mysterious Underpinnings of Emotional Life*. Weidenfeld and Nicolson.

McFarlane, A.C. (1988) The longitudinal course of post-traumatic morbidity, the range about cones and their predictors. *Journal of Nervous and Mental Diseases*, 176: 30–39.

Meichenbaum, D. (1985) *Stress Inoculation Training*. London: Pergamon Press.

Mueser, K.T., Goodman, S.L., Trumbetta, S.D., Rosenberg, S.D., Osher, F.C., Vidaver, R. et al. (1998) Trauma and post-traumatic stress disorder in severe mental illness. *Journal of Consulting and Clinical Psychology*, 66: 493–499.

Otis, J.D., Keane, T.M. and Kerns, R.D. (2003) An examination of the relationship between chronic pain and post-traumatic stress disorder. *Journal of Rehabilitation and Development*, 40: 397–406.

Padesky, C.A. and Greenberg, D. (1995) *Clinician's Guide to Mind Over Mood*. New York: Guilford Press.

Resick, P.A. and Schnicke, M.K. (1993) *Cognitive Processing Therapy for Rape Victims*. Newbury Park, CA: Sage.

Rothbaum, B.O. and Foa, E.B. (1993) Subtypes of PTSD and duration of symptoms, in J.R.T. Davidson and E.B. Foa (eds) *PTSD: DSM IV and Beyond*. Washington, DC: American Psychiatric Press.

Rothbaum, B.O., Foa, E.B., Riggs, D.S., Murdock, T. and Walsh, W. (1992) A prospective examination of PTSD in rape victim. *Journal of Traumatic Stress*, 5: 455–475.

Scheeringa, M.S., Zeanah, C.H., Myers, L. and Putnam, F.W. (2003) New findings on alternative criteria for PTSD in preschool children. *Journal of the American Academy of Child and Adolescent Psychiatry*, 42: 561–570.

Scott, M.J. and Sembi, S. (2002) Unreliable assessment in civil litigation. *The Psychologist*, 15: 80–81.

Scott, M.J. and Sembi, S. (2006) Cognitive behavioural treatment failures in practice: the neglected role of diagnostic accuracy. *Behavioural and Cognitive Psychotherapy*, 34: 491–495.

Scott, M.J. and Stradling, S.G. (1994) Post-traumatic stress disorder without the trauma. *British Journal of Clinical Psychology*, 33: 71–74.

Scott, M.J. and Stradling, S.G. (2000) Trauma, stress and duress, in N. Tehrani (ed.) *Building a Culture of Respect: Managing Bullying at Work*. London: Taylor and Francis.

Scott, M.J. and Stradling, S.G. (2006) *Counselling for Post-Traumatic Stress Disorder*, 3rd edn. London: Sage.

Shapiro, F. (1995) *Eye Movement Desensitisation and Reprocessing: Basic Principles, Protocols, and Procedures*. New York: Guilford Press.

Wells, A. and Sembi, S. (2004) Metacognitive therapy for PTSD: A core treatment manual. *Cognitive and Behavioral Practice*, 11: 365–377.

Zimmerman, M. and Mattia, J.I. (1999) Psychiatric diagnoses in clinical practice: Is comorbidity being missed? *Comprehensive Psychiatry*, 40: 182–191.

Index

Abigail – 6-year old child,
    post-traumatic stress disorder 20,
    31, 48, 51, 62, 84, 151, 153–6
Acceptance and Commitment
    Therapy 126
active scheduling 144
adolescents 19, 153, 156–7, 171
agencies 167–8
agoraphobia 12, 13, 19, 145, 181
alcohol use 12, 67, 133, 138–40;
    cognitive behavioural therapy 43;
    as coping strategy 63; internal
    critical voice 55; sleep problems
    129
Amanda – 14-year old suffering
    from body dysmorphic disorder
    20–1, 25, 62, 80, 84, 151,
    156–7
amygdala 26–7, 32, 46, 53–4, 90, 91;
    hippocampus interaction with
    29–30, 33; panic attacks 58, 148;
    sensitisation 37, 38
Angela – depression and post-
    traumatic stress disorder
    following physical and sexual
    abuse in childhood and
    adolescence 9–11; avoidance 47,
    54; mood management 117–18;
    treatment 165; writing about the
    trauma 75
anger 41, 90–3, 97, 117; cognitive
    behavioural therapy 39; DSM-IV-
    TR diagnostic criteria 177;
    focusing on the right target 118;
    see also irritability

anniversaries of trauma 6
Anthony – 3-year old child,
    traumatic stress reaction 20, 31,
    151, 152–3, 155
antidepressants 39, 42, 163, 166
anxiety 37, 152, 153, 181
anxiety disorders 12–13, 18, 37, 39;
    see also generalised anxiety
    disorder; social anxiety
'approach' 47–9, 170
Armed Services 167
arousal 177
assault victims 9, 14, 34, 77, 83
attention training 68
automatic discounting 98, 99
avoidance 7, 11, 41, 46–7, 170;
    agoraphobic 12, 19, 145; Angela's
    case 54; DSM-IV-TR diagnostic
    criteria 177; Kevin's case 52;
    Peter's case 60; Sam's case 32;
    social anxiety 89; talking about
    the trauma 69

BABCP see British Association for
    Behavioural and Cognitive
    Psychotherapies
Beck, Aaron 40
bed-wetting 152
beliefs 32
biases in thinking 98–101, 122–3,
    124, 143
Blanchard, E.B. 34–5
Bob – prolonged duress stress
    disorder after bullying at work
    19, 61; anger 41, 90–1; prejudice

against self 104; traumatic memories 67, 68
bodily sensations 63, 70, 148
body dysmorphic disorder 21, 23, 108, 112
borderline personality disorder 15
brain: control-demand system 30–1, 33; threat evaluation system 29–31, 33; traumatic memories 65; *see also* amygdala
brain injury 16–17, 113, 115
Breslau, N. 37
Brewin, Chris 9, 35–6, 174
British Association for Behavioural and Cognitive Psychotherapies (BABCP) 158, 165, 167
broken record technique 115
bulimia 108
bullying 19, 67, 104
Butler, A.C. 39

catastrophisation 123
CBT *see* cognitive behavioural therapy
Cecilia – PTSD after road traffic accident 20–1, 22, 25–7, 62; avoidance 46–7; children's reaction to trauma 151, 152–7; cognitive behavioural therapy 40; Communication Guidelines 86–9; land of approach 48–9; litigation 160; nightmares 132; obsessive compulsive disorder 140–1; recovery prospects 34, 35; relationship issues 84–5; threat evaluation system 29–30, 31; training schedule 49–51; writing about the trauma 80
Chapman, Robin 115
charities 167
childhood abuse 9, 11, 15, 36–7, 134; *see also* physical abuse; sexual abuse
children 19–21, 151–6, 171, 176, 179
CICA *see* Criminal Injury Compensation Authority
co-morbidity 37, 133
cognitive behavioural therapy (CBT) 39–43, 45, 94, 165, 167; Angela's case 165; high expressed emotion impact on 137; John's

case 163, 164; Karen's case 162; NHS waiting lists for 158; Sandra's case 17, 113
cognitive contextual therapy 41, 170–1
cognitive processing therapy 41
cognitive restructuring 30, 115
Columbo 3
Combat Stress 167
Communication Guidelines 86–9
compensation 78–9, 85, 158, 161, 164, 167
concentration 1, 8, 16; adolescents 156; depression 144, 145; DSM-IV-TR diagnostic criteria 177, 179
conspiracy of silence 3
control-demand system 30–1, 33
coping self-statements 112–17, 128
coping strategies 40–1, 65, 114, 170; alcohol problems 139–40; childhood abuse 134; ineffective 63–4, 66
counselling 3–4, 36, 167; CBT comparison 41–2; guidance for professionals 169, 170; occupational health service 104, 166
Criminal Injury Compensation Authority (CICA) 75, 78, 79, 162, 167
critical voice 54–6

danger signs 5
'dares' 49–54, 58–61, 73, 156
daydreaming 7–8, 131
defendant's insurers 163, 167
depression 37, 94, 110, 144–6; Angela's case 9–11, 165; brain injury 16; cognitive behavioural therapy 39, 42–3; DSM-IV-TR diagnostic criteria 178–80; expert witness reports 163; high expressed emotion 137; Jack's case 18; Joan's case 12; Karen's case 15; loss of valued role 104; Patrick's case 12, 82, 105; Peter's case 13
detached mindfulness 42, 58, 66, 67, 68, 129
diagnosis 175

Diagnostic and Statistical Manual (DSM-IV-TR) 18, 176–81; children 19, 152; depression 178–80; panic disorder 180–1; PTSD diagnostic criteria 90, 176–8; social phobia 89; trauma-related guilt 13
dichotomous thinking 99, 100, 111
dissociative flashbacks 6, 63, 177, 178
'dodgy alarm' 25–7, 48–9, 56, 58, 148
dreams 73–4, 131, 176; *see also* nightmares
drug abuse 12, 37
DSM-IV-TR *see Diagnostic and Statistical Manual*
dysthymic disorder 15, 78

EMDR *see* eye movement desensitisation and reprocessing
Emma – PTSD after tripping whilst pregnant and later panic disorder with moderate agoraphobic avoidance 18–19, 61–2, 148–50
emotional disorder 13–14, 37
emotional intelligence 87, 89, 95–6, 137
emotional numbness 5, 28–9, 32; DSM-IV-TR diagnostic criteria 177; John's case 96–7; Kevin's case 40
emotional reasoning 98, 99
emotions: anger 90–3; background 91, 136–7; cognitive contextual therapy 41; exposure therapy 70; high levels of expressed 137; impaired affect modulation 15, 178; labelling 72; mood management 117–18; Pedro's case 67; writing about the trauma 81
employers 97, 163–4, 166
escape 7, 11
expert witnesses 158–9, 161–3, 167
exposure therapy 41, 45, 70–1
eye movement desensitisation and reprocessing (EMDR) 39, 43–5, 66, 165

family 2–3, 43
fatigue 179
fear 27, 51, 62, 176
fire-fighters 34

flashbacks 6, 9–11, 41, 63, 177; detached mindfulness 42; Kevin's case 40; Pedro's case 67; Peter's case 81; Sam's case 32; talking about the trauma 73, 74; toxic accompaniments to dares 54, 58, 59–60, 61; *see also* memories
friends 2–3, 43, 142, 143

general practitioners (GPs) 138, 139–40, 158, 163, 166
generalised anxiety disorder 13, 36, 39, 146–7; *see also* anxiety disorders
goals 126–7
GPs *see* general practitioners
Group Parent Training Programme 153, 154, 155
group treatment 172
guilt 9, 11, 13, 98–100, 179

habituation 71
hallucinations 37, 177
Hansen, Alan 109
helplessness 7–8, 29, 151; catastrophisation 123; DSM-IV-TR diagnostic criteria 176; narrating the trauma 71, 72
Hickling, E. 34–5
hippocampus 29–30, 33
hopelessness 108, 178
humour 93, 117
hyperarousal 5, 8–9, 32, 177
hypervigilance 177

Ian – shot at work, pain a major problem as well as PTSD 14, 36; coping self-statements 113; negative self-description 56; nightmares 131; pain 120, 121, 125–6, 127–8; rereading of trauma statement 78–9; sleep problems 119–20, 121, 129–30
identity crisis 5
imagery 127–8, 139
impaired affect modulation 15, 178
information processing: arrested 71; biases in thinking 98–101, 122–3, 124, 143
insurers 163, 167
internal critical voice 54–6

intrusions 6–7, 26–7, 165; detached mindfulness 66; DSM-IV-TR diagnostic criteria 176; toxic accompaniments to dares 58; *see also* flashbacks; re-experiencing
irritability 40, 90, 91, 118; adolescents 156; DSM-IV-TR diagnostic criteria 177; sleep problems 129, 130, 131; *see also* anger
isolation 31–2, 84, 168

Jack – already existing mild learning difficulties and anxiety disorder not otherwise specified after a pedestrian road traffic accident 18, 115–17
Joan – panic disorder and severe agoraphobic avoidance and depression after being mugged 12, 58–9; coping strategy 40–1; depression 145–6; high expressed emotion 137
John – PTSD and depression as a result of a gas explosion at work 22–3; depression 144–5; flashbacks 59–60; litigation 162–4; mood 96–8; nightmares 131–2; talking about the trauma 74
journals 80
jumping to conclusions 99, 124
justice 158–64

Karen – PTSD and social phobia following rape and dysthymic disorder following childhood sexual abuse 15–16, 36; background emotion 136–7; biases in thinking 101; expert witness report 161–2; negative self-description 56–7; prejudice against self 102; recovery prospects 34; rereading of trauma statement 77–8; sleep problems 128–9; social phobia 142, 143; timeline 134–6; updating of early memory 136
Kevin – PTSD and trauma-related guilt after being assaulted 9, 40; avoidance 46; biases in thinking 100–1; coping strategy 41;

internal critical voice 54–5; relationship issues 85–6; rereading of trauma statement 77; social anxiety 89, 90; training schedule 52–3

labelling 99
Ladbroke Grove train crash 174
learning difficulties 17–18
litigation 158–64
London bombings (2005) 174
loss of valued role 104–6

magnification 99, 123
marriage issues 84, 85, 86, 87–8
massage 17
Maureen – phobia about getting on a bus and generalised anxiety disorder 11, 36; internal critical voice 55–6; key ideas 146–7
McFarlane, A.C. 34
Meichenbaum, Donald 112, 128
memories 6, 32–3, 171; acknowledging at a distance 66–8; bully analogy 64–5; dictating the story of the trauma 70–5; handling 63–4; mood management 94; rereading of trauma statement 77, 78; rumination 68–9; updating of early memory 136; writing about the trauma 81; *see also* flashbacks
mental filter 99, 101, 109
metacognitive therapy 41
mindfulness 42, 58, 66, 67, 68, 129
minimisation 99
mislabelling 99
mood 11, 78, 94–118, 171; alcohol impact on 129; biases in thinking 98–101; broad investment portfolio 110–11; coping self-statements 112–17; loss of valued role 104–6; monitoring 145; pain relationship 119, 123; prejudice against self 101–4; recovery from depression 144; replacing emotions 117–18; role impairment 106–10; rumination 122; thought record 95–8; timetabling uplifts 111–12

MOOD framework 95–6, 115, 124; Ian's case 120, 121; Joan's case 145–6; John's case 97; Karen's case 143; Maureen's case 147; Tessa's case 122, 123
Mueser, K.T. 37

National Health Service (NHS) 158, 165, 166, 167
negative self-descriptions 54, 56–8, 99, 101–4
NHS *see* National Health Service
nightmares 6, 8, 22, 63; children 153, 154; rescripting 131–2; talking about the trauma 73–4; toxic accompaniments to dares 58

obsessive compulsive disorder (OCD) 13, 20, 140–1
occupational health service 104, 166
OCD *see* obsessive compulsive disorder
over-generalisation 99, 124

pacing 126–7
pain 13–14, 22, 119, 120–8; cognitive behavioural therapy 39; goals and pacing 126–7; imagery 127–8; monitoring 120, 121, 124–6; Self Instruction Training 128; unhelpful thinking about 122–4
panic attacks 12, 18–19, 148–9; coping strategies 40–1; DSM-IV-TR diagnostic criteria 180, 181; toxic accompaniments to dares 54, 58
panic disorder 13, 19, 37, 148–50; amygdala role 27; cognitive behavioural therapy 39; DSM-IV-TR diagnostic criteria 180–1; Joan's case 12, 40, 145
Patrick – depression after falling off scaffolding 11–12; broad investment portfolio 111; internal critical voice 55; litigation 160–1; loss of valued role 104–6; mood management 117; pacing 127; timetabling uplifts 112; writing about the trauma 82
PDSD *see* prolonged duress stress disorder

Pedro – physically abused in childhood, PTSD and associated symptoms of PTSD and depression 15; anger 91–2; negative self-description 57; traumatic memories 66–7, 68–9
'performance gaps' 106, 110
personalisation 98, 99
Peter – trauma-related guilt, PTSD, depression after trying to help a man who fell from scaffolding 13; biases in thinking 98–100; flashbacks 60; writing about the trauma 81–2
phobia 11, 13, 36; cognitive behavioural therapy 43; internal critical voice 55–6; *see also* social phobia
'photocopy' of trauma 79, 80
physical abuse 15, 38, 57, 165; *see also* childhood abuse
physiotherapy 127
post-traumatic stress disorder (PTSD): additional disorders 12–14, 37–8; alcohol abuse 138; amygdala role 27, 89–90; arrested information processing 71; borderline cases 18–19; children 20, 151–2, 153; depression 144; DSM-IV-TR diagnostic criteria 176–8; emotional numbness 28–9; fears 51; generalised anxiety disorder 146; impact on relationships 83; irritability 90, 118; life in a 'bubble' 27–8, 83; obsessive compulsive disorder 140; panic disorder 148; persistence 32–3; recovery 34–8, 39; repeated traumas 14–16; social phobia 142; symptoms of 6–9, 176–8; Trauma Screening Questionnaire 9–11, 173–4; treatment 39, 165; unreliable diagnosis 175
pre-school children 151–3
prejudice against self 101–4, 126, 134–5
Present Pain Intensity Scale 124–5
professional guidance 169–72
prolonged duress stress disorder (PDSD) 19, 91

psychomotor agitation 179
psychosis 37, 38
PTSD *see* post-traumatic stress
disorder

rape 15–16, 57, 101; background
emotions 137; recovery of victims
34; rereading of trauma
statement 77–8; sleep problems
128; *see also* sexual abuse
re-experiencing 6–7, 32, 63, 70, 176–7
reassurance 51
recovery 34–8, 39, 137, 168
referential activity 79
reflexive adaptive processing 66
regression 20
relationships 83–93, 170–1; anger
90–3; Communication Guidelines
86–9; reinvesting 84–6; social
anxiety 89–90
relaxation exercises 147
religion 168
reminders 6, 7, 26–7
repeated traumas 14–16
rereading the traumatic story 75–9
'responsibility pie' 135, 157
road traffic accidents 5–6, 34, 35, 83
Role Performance Questionnaire
106, 107–8, 109
role-playing 114, 116
roles: broad investment portfolio
110–11; loss of valued role 104–6;
performance 106–10, 146
Rothbaum, B.O. 34
rumination 7–8, 68–9, 171;
depressive 111, 146; impact on
mood 122; pain 123

saboteurs 54–62
'safe place' 28, 31, 44, 56
'safety' behaviours 54, 140, 150
Sam – probable PTSD following road
traffic accident and drink
problem 5–6; alcohol abuse 12, 55,
67, 133, 138–40; anger 92–3;
flashbacks 32, 41; internal critical
voice 55; negative beliefs 32;
prejudice against self 103;
recovery prospects 35;
rumination 7–8; timeline 133–4;
traumatic memories 33, 67–8, 69

Sandra – mild brain injury following
a climbing accident 16–17; coping
self-statements 113–15; negative
self-description 57–8; role
performance 106; talking about
the trauma 69–70
Scheeringa, M.S. 152
schizophrenia 37, 137
Scott, M.J. 19, 38
selective abstraction 124
self-blame 94, 100, 101–2, 103, 118,
134
self-consciousness 112
self-esteem 108, 133
self-injury 14, 57
Self Instruction Training (SIT)
112–13, 115, 128–9
self-statements 112–17
Sembi, S. 66
sexual abuse 9, 11, 14, 15–16, 134,
165; avoidance 47; expert witness
reports 161–2; psychotic women
38; sleep problems 129; *see also*
rape
Shapiro, Francine 43
'should' statements 99, 100
SIT *see* Self Instruction Training
sleep 63, 80, 119–20, 121; diary
129–30; DSM-IV-TR diagnostic
criteria 177, 179; rescripting
nightmares 131–2; Self
Instruction Training 128–9; *see
also* nightmares
social anxiety 84, 89–90
social interactions 36, 143
social phobia 13, 16, 39, 84, 89–90,
142–3
social support 36, 168, 170–1
somatic disorders 39, 178
standardised approaches 171,
175
startle response 177
'stop-think-act' approach 145–6
'stop-think-relax' technique 17,
115–17
Stradling, S.G. 19, 38
stress: litigation 160–1; recovery
from PTSD 36
subjective units of distress (SUDS)
76, 78
substance abuse 12, 37

SUDS *see* subjective units of
    distress
suicide 179

talking about trauma 69–70
temper tantrums 154
Tessa – body dysmorphic disorder,
    mild brain injury, pain and
    depression since riding accident
    23; MOOD framework 122, 123;
    pain 120–2; role performance
    108–10
thinking biases 98–101, 122–3, 124,
    143
thought record 95–8, 147
threat evaluation system 29–31, 33,
    91
thumbnail sketch of trauma 21–2
traffic light strategy 92–3
training schedules: Cecilia 49–51;
    Kevin 52–3
trauma discrimination 61

trauma map 26
trauma-related guilt 9, 11, 13, 98–100
Trauma Screening Questionnaire
    (TSQ) 9–11, 14, 21, 173–4

uncertainty 100

vertigo 76
Victim Support Service 168
video surveillance 160–1
visual aids 17

'war zone' 26, 31, 46, 49, 51, 54,
    91
weight loss 179
Wells, A. 66
Weston, Simon 82
work performance 8
workplace counselling 104, 166
writing about the trauma 79–82;
    Angela's case 75; rereading the
    account 75–9